T0129082

The Windows 10 Productivity Handbook

Discover Expert Tips, Tricks, and Hidden Features in Windows 10

Mike Halsey

Apress®

The Windows 10 Productivity Handbook

Mike Halsey
Sheffield, Yorkshire, UK

ISBN-13 (pbk): 978-1-4842-3293-4   ISBN-13 (electronic): 978-1-4842-3294-1
https://doi.org/10.1007/978-1-4842-3294-1

Library of Congress Control Number: 2017960182

Managing Director: Welmoed Spahr
Editorial Director: Todd Green
Acquisitions Editor: Gwenan Spearing
Development Editor: Laura Berendson
Technical Reviewer: Ralph Mercurio
Coordinating Editor: Nancy Chen
Copy Editor: Kim Burton-Weisman
Compositor: SPi Global
Indexer: SPi Global
Artist: SPi Global

Distributed to the book trade worldwide by Springer Science+Business Media New York, 233 Spring Street, 6th Floor, New York, NY 10013. Phone 1-800-SPRINGER, fax (201) 348-4505, e-mail orders-ny@springer-sbm.com, or visit www.springeronline.com. Apress Media, LLC is a California LLC and the sole member (owner) is Springer Science + Business Media Finance Inc (SSBM Finance Inc). SSBM Finance Inc is a **Delaware** corporation.

For information on translations, please e-mail rights@apress.com, or visit http://www.apress.com/rights-permissions.

Apress titles may be purchased in bulk for academic, corporate, or promotional use. eBook versions and licenses are also available for most titles. For more information, reference our Print and eBook Bulk Sales web page at http://www.apress.com/bulk-sales.

Any source code or other supplementary material referenced by the author in this book is available to readers on GitHub via the book's product page, located at www.apress.com/9781484232934. For more detailed information, please visit http://www.apress.com/source-code.

Printed on acid-free paper

Contents at a Glance

About the Author xi

About the Technical Reviewer xiii

■Chapter 1: Getting Up to Speed with Windows 10 1

■Chapter 2: Making Your PC More Pleasurable to Use 13

■Chapter 3: Achieving More with Windows 10 23

■Chapter 4: Productivity Boost Tips and Tricks 37

■Chapter 5: Maximize Your Windows Experience 47

■Chapter 6: Using Search to Keep Yourself Organized 55

■Chapter 7: Managing Windows Settings and Configuration 67

■Chapter 8: Managing Network Connections and Devices 79

■Chapter 9: Keeping Yourself and Your Data Safe and Secure 89

■Chapter 10: Maintaining a Stable and Reliable Working Environment 99

■Appendix A: Windows 10 Shortcut Keys 111

■Appendix B: Windows 10 Touch and Trackpad Gestures 115

■Appendix C: Advanced Query Syntax for Search 119

Index 127

Contents

About the Author xi

About the Technical Reviewer xiii

◼Chapter 1: Getting Up to Speed with Windows 10 1

Getting Familiar with Windows 10 1

    The Windows 10 Desktop 2

    App Tiles in the Start Menu 4

    A Visit to the Taskbar 5

    Work Longer in Windows 10 7

Finding and Understanding Settings 8

Summary 11

◼Chapter 2: Making Your PC More Pleasurable to Use 13

Personalizing the Lock Screen 13

Making Windows 10 Easier on the Eye 14

    Changing the Desktop Wallpaper 14

    Changing Colors 15

Making Text and On-Screen Items Easier to Read and Use 17

Changing Region Settings for the PC 20

That Syncing Feeling 22

Summary 22

▓**Chapter 3: Achieving More with Windows 10** **23**

Cortana: Much More Than a Personal Assistant 23

    Intelligent Reminders 24

    Connected to Everything 25

    Then There's Everything Else 25

Windows Ink 25

Snap! 27

Working with Virtual Desktops 29

Pick Up Where You Left Off with Timeline 31

Managing Printers in Windows 10 32

Using OneDrive Files On-Demand 33

    Using OneDrive File Versioning 34

Summary 35

▓**Chapter 4: Productivity Boost Tips and Tricks** **37**

Shake It All About! 37

Taking a Quick Peek 37

Keeping Things Quiet 38

    Manage Your Quick Actions Buttons 41

Smart Search 42

Managing Battery Life and Background Apps 45

    Using the Mobility Center 46

Summary 46

▓**Chapter 5: Maximize Your Windows Experience** **47**

Getting Your Day Started 47

Organizing Your Workspace 49

    Managing Virtual Desktops 50

Where the Heck Did I Put that Report? 51

    Hey, Cortana… Where the Heck Did I Put that Report? 52

Summary 54

■Chapter 6: Using Search to Keep Yourself Organized 55

Using Saved Searches in Windows 10 56

Configuring Search in Windows 10 56

Organizing Your Files Using Libraries 58

　　Managing File and Document Tags and Details.. 61

Sharing Files and Documents 62

Managing the Quick Access View.. 63

　　Pinning Folders to Quick Access.. 65

Summary... 65

■Chapter 7: Managing Windows Settings and Configuration 67

The Settings Panel 67

System Settings 69

　　Making Your Display Easier to Use 69

　　Managing Notifications.. 70

　　Power to the People! 72

Keep Taking the Tablets!... 76

How to Win at Snap!.. 76

Summary... 77

■Chapter 8: Managing Network Connections and Devices....................................... 79

Managing Hardware Devices 79

　　Managing Your Default Printers... 79

　　Managing USB Device AutoPlay... 80

Network and Internet 82

　　Managing Wi-Fi Networks 82

　　Managing VPN Connections.. 83

　　Additional Network Settings... 84

Apps and Features 85

　　Making Your PC More Secure 85

　　Default Apps 86

Accounts..87

Summary..88

▓**Chapter 9: Keeping Yourself and Your Data Safe and Secure 89**

Surely, I Just Install Antivirus… Right?!...89

How Do Malware Infections Happen?...90

How Does Hacking Happen? 92

Crikey! What Else Should I Look Out For?..92

Okay, Now My Head Hurts! How Do I Stay Safe?...................................93

Keep Everything Up-to-Date 93

Use Strong Passwords and Two-Factor Authentication..................................96

Don't Just Click Anything Online! 96

Don't Click Anything in Your Email Either! 97

Safety and Security Are Common Sense...98

Summary..98

▓**Chapter 10: Maintaining a Stable and Reliable Working Environment...............99**

If It Ain't Broke, Don't Fix It...99

Taming Windows Update 99

Sleeping at Work..101

Pausing and Deferring Updates..104

Using the Automated Troubleshooters..105

System Restore 106

Creating a Windows 10 Recovery Drive 107

Summary..109

▓**Appendix A: Windows 10 Shortcut Keys 111**

▓**Appendix B: Windows 10 Touch and Trackpad Gestures 115**

Narrator Touch Gestures..116

Trackpad Gestures...117

■Appendix C: Advanced Query Syntax for Search **119**

Data Store Location 119

Common File Types 120

Properties by File Type 121

Filter by Size 121

Boolean Operators 122

Boolean Properties 122

Dates 123

Attachments 123

Contacts 124

Communications 125

Calendar 125

Documents 125

Presentations 126

Music 126

Pictures 126

Video 126

Index **127**

About the Author

Mike Halsey was first awarded as a Microsoft Most Valuable Professional (MVP) in 2011. He is the author of more than a dozen Windows books, including *Windows 10 Troubleshooting* (Apress, 2016), *Beginning Windows 10* (Apress, 2015), and *The Windows 10 Accessibility Handbook* (Apress, 2015). He is also the Series Editor and an author for Apress' Windows and Windows Server Troubleshooting books.

Based in Sheffield, UK, where he lives with his rescue border collies, Evan and Robbie, he gives many talks on Windows subjects—from productivity to security, and makes how-to and troubleshooting videos under the banners PCSupport.tv and Windows.do. You can follow him on Facebook and Twitter at @MikeHalsey.

About the Technical Reviewer

 **Ralph Mercurio** is a director with Capeless Solutions, which focuses on Microsoft 365 and SharePoint in the areas of infrastructure, development, and migration. Ralph has over 13 years of experience working in technology in a variety of roles and across many industries.

CHAPTER 1

▓ ▓▓ ▓

Getting Up to Speed with Windows 10

Do you dream? Do you watch people around you going about their daily tasks, and wonder how they're able to achieve things you can't, be more effective than you can be, or have more time for enjoyment? You're not alone: at some point, everybody will have watched another person achieve what they would consider to be almost impossible.

This happens on a macro level when we see explorers heading into the vast unknowns of the Arctic or the Himalayas. It happens when we watch extreme sports or when someone's latest app has just made them their first million at age 21. It also happens on the micro level when you visit a friend and see just how beautiful and colorful their garden is, or just how they're able to prepare and cook such an amazingly tasty meal from exotic ingredients you've never heard of.

This feeling isn't just restricted to our private lives either. In the workplace, we have all watched a colleague do something, manually or with their PC, that seems to elevate their own work above the people around them, or that saves them huge amounts of time, enabling them to do more, or to a higher standard than you yourself know how.

We all want to be more productive and effective at what we do. Our employers want it, our clients want it, and we want it for ourselves. It makes our work engaging and more understandable, while making us more employable and giving us greater self-esteem.

While I'm afraid I can't help you with either cooking or gardening (much as I wish I could), I *can* help you with your use of Windows 10 at home, at college, and in the workplace.

This book is your cheat sheet, your masterclass, and your easy-to-follow guide on how to achieve those things on your PC that you've seen others do, but that you don't have a clue how to do yourself.

▓ **Note**   Microsoft regularly updates and refines Windows 10, just as apps are regularly updated. This means that some features or functionality might look different from that described here, or may change slightly after a period of time. It also means that new features or functionality might be added. Fundamentally, however, Microsoft will not change the overall function or discoverability of the operating system or your apps.

Getting Familiar with Windows 10

Windows 10 seems like the logical place to begin this journey. It's the workspace in which everything happens, the container for your apps and files, and the thing you'll spend the vast amount of your time interacting with.

© Mike Halsey 2017
M. Halsey, *The Windows 10 Productivity Handbook*, https://doi.org/10.1007/978-1-4842-3294-1_1

Let's begin by looking at the *lock screen* because it's the first thing you see when you start your PC. In the center of the lock screen is your user photo or avatar, below which is a box asking you for your PIN or password if you have one set up on the PC (see Figure 1-1).

Figure 1-1. *The lock screen contains useful options*

You can switch between different sign-in methods (PIN, password, and Windows Hello) by clicking the sign-in options. This can be useful because sometimes you might find Windows 10 switches to asking you for a password, when you'd rather sign in with a PIN.

If there is more than one user account configured on the PC, you will see a list of available users listed in the bottom-left corner of the lock screen. You can click a user icon to sign in to the PC as that user instead of the one currently shown in the center of the screen.

In the bottom-right corner of the screen are icons for your network connection (should you need to connect to Wi-Fi), *Ease of Access* (if you need to make Windows 10 easier to use when you sign in), and *Power* (so you can shut down and restart the PC directly from the lock screen).

The Windows 10 Desktop

When you sign in to Windows, you are presented with the Windows 10 desktop—what it offers and how to become accustomed to it. If you look at your own desktop, what do you see? You'll very likely see the *Start menu* and the *taskbar* that runs across the bottom of the screen (see Figure 1-2).

Figure 1-2. *The Windows 10 desktop and Start menu*

Do you see the other features that can save you time and make you more productive? Because as there are actually more than you might think. Pressing either the Windows icon in the bottom-right corner of the screen or the Windows key on your keyboard opens the Start menu. In the bottom-left corner of the Start menu are icons to sign out of your user account, open Settings (which I'll cover later in this chapter), and restart and shut down the PC.

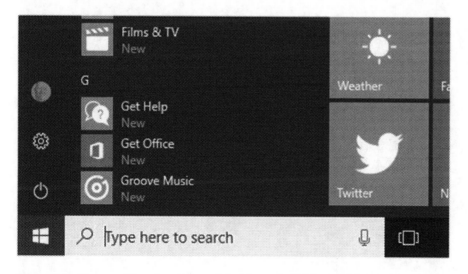

Figure 1-3. *You can sign out, restart, and shut down the PC from the Start menu, see Figure 1-4*

Clicking your user or the Power icon displays a pop-up menu containing additional options from which you can choose. If you're ever unsure what it what, clicking the "hamburger menu," which is the three horizontal lines in the top-left corner of the Start menu displays text descriptions of what each button does.

App Tiles in the Start Menu

Most of us are used to using apps on our smartphones and tablets. Windows 10 isn't any stranger to apps, having an extensive library available in the Microsoft Store. You'll see these apps listed in the alphabetical app list to the left of the Start menu, but also pinned to the Start menu itself.

There are different things you can do with these apps, and several ways in which they can help you. At their most basic, they can act as a quick glance way to get access to information. Most apps display content from within the app itself, such as the details of recently received emails, calendar appointments, news or sports headlines, or financial information, directly on the tile itself.

The advantage of this is that you can, just through pressing the Windows key on your keyboard, check at a glance if there's anything new, and if it should be opened and dealt with straightaway, or if it can wait for a while.

These *live tiles* can also help you prevent having to open and use the app itself. If you're waiting to see that the shares in the company you just bought are doing when the market opens, a live tile can give you this information. All at the same time and in the same space on your screen as you can see the latest weather forecast, social media updates, private message, and more besides.

For some people, this might be considered a distraction. After all, you might have a Facebook app, or a sports app installed, but you don't want to be distracted by what's going on. By right-clicking a tile, you can turn the live functionality on or off (see Figure 1-4). Additionally, you can change the tile through four different sizes, small, medium, wide, and large, so they take up more (or less) space as you see fit, drag them around the Start menu to rearrange them, or even remove them from the Start menu (unpin them) or uninstall them altogether. All of this is achieved on the same right-click (or a touch-and-hold on your touchscreen device).

Figure 1-4. *You can turn live tile functionality on or off*

The Start menu itself can be customized. If you drag its top or right edges, you can make it larger of smaller. If you right-click the taskbar along the bottom of your screen, a taskbar settings option will appear (see Figure 1-5). This opens the Settings panel, in which you see customization options for the taskbar, and to the left of the panel, a link to customization options for the Start menu.

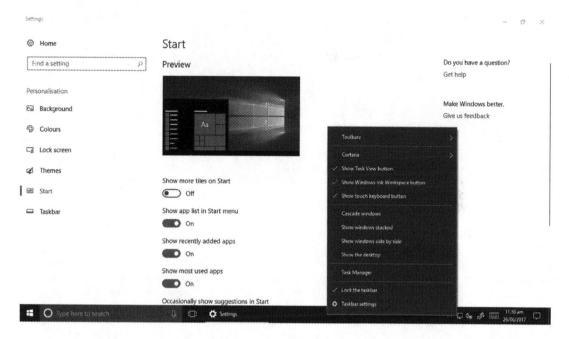

Figure 1-5. *You can customize the Start menu and taskbar*

You can customize many different aspects of the Start menu, including your most used apps, most recently used apps, and suggestions for new apps—by which Microsoft mean advertisements. You can easily turn off these suggestions.

A Visit to the Taskbar

Beneath the desktop and Start menu sits the taskbar. You'll probably know this as the place where the icons for your open apps sit, but it's capable of being much more than that. For example, you can right-click (touch and hold) any icon to rampantly pin (or unpin) it from the taskbar. This can make it easier and faster to open the apps you want to use.

Additionally, right-clicking an icon can reveal a pop-up *Jump List*. This provides additional context-sensitive functionality (see Figure 1-6). The File Explorer Jump List provides quick links to various folders on your PC, the Outlook Jump List contains quick links to new emails, appointments, and contacts, and an app Jump List can provide quick links to your most recently used files.

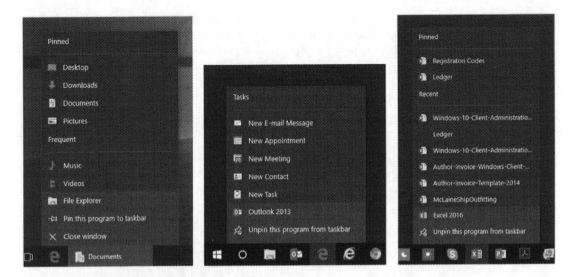

Figure 1-6. *Jump Lists provide useful additional functionality*

Files can also be pinned to Jump Lists so that they're always available. As you move your mouse up and down the list of recently opened files, you'll see a "pin" icon appear to the right of each one. You can click this to pin (or unpin) any file, just as you can with apps on the Start menu. This means that crucial project or regularly used files are available to you with a quick click, no matter what else you've been doing.

To the right of the taskbar sits the *system tray*. You'll recognize that this includes the clock and the current date. There's more here than meets the eye, however.

You'll see an icon that looks like a speech balloon on the very far-right side of the taskbar. This is the Action Center (see Figure 1-7). It contains additional quick links and all of your received and app notifications.

Figure 1-7. *On the right side of the taskbar sits the system tray*

Each notification is grouped, so you can see all the notifications from one app together, such as received emails or security notifications. You can dismiss a notification by clicking the X to its top right, or by swiping it off your screen with your finger or mouse.

At the bottom of the Action Center are the quick actions buttons. These include some incredibly useful gems such as *Quiet Hours,* which automatically silences all audio and pop-up notifications, enabling you to concentrate on work or your important presentation without distraction.

The *Note* icon takes you directly to Microsoft OneNote so you can organize your thoughts (more on OneNote later in this book). A *project* icon can help you quickly connect to and find the right presentation mode for a projector.

Night Light changes the color temperature of your screen, making it less of a strain on your eyes if you're working in the evening. *Airplane mode* enables you to quickly make your mobile device safe when you're on a red-eye flight to Seattle, and *Tablet mode* allows you to quickly switch between keyboard and mouse, and touch interfaces for the desktop and your running apps.

The system tray also contains additional icons, some part of Windows, and some for your running apps. There are icons to display an on-screen keyboard, check the status of your network connection, and control the volume of your PC. Additionally, you see a small up arrow (^), which, when clicked, contains a bucket of hidden icons. You might find your antivirus software in here, so you can check its status, or a useful app you have running in the background for which you want to change the settings.

These system tray icons can be rearranged, hidden, and unhidden by simply dragging them to where you want them to be. You can also control them on a more granular level by opening the taskbar settings, as demonstrated in Figure 1-5, and navigating to the *Notification area* section on the taskbar settings page. Here you find controls to *Select which icons appear on the taskbar* and *Turn system icons on or off.*

Work Longer in Windows 10

What?! I hear you cry. You're supposed to be helping make me become more productive and give me more time playing with the kids and walking the dog, and in the first chapter you're already telling me how I can work for longer?!

Panic ye not, as there's a hidden little trick with Windows apps that extends the battery life on your PC, enabling you to get through an entire working day without having to tether yourself to the mains, or to allow you the extra power you need to watch that new Netflix episode when you're done.

Everything on a PC uses electricity, and that means on a mobile device such as a laptop or tablet, everything uses battery power. If you install what you might call a "traditional application" on your PC, which is anything and everything that *doesn't* come from the Microsoft Store, it makes the processor and memory in the PC do stuff, which uses power.

If you minimize that application, or put it to the background so you can do something else, it's still running, still doing stuff, and still using power.

However, anything that is installed from the Microsoft Store behaves differently in that when it is minimized or put in the background it is suspended. In this suspended state, it uses little or no power, thus extending the battery life of your PC.

If you use a lot of apps in windows scattered around your desktop, the PC uses more power still, as the graphics engine has to draw, and keep up to date, every individual window. Maximizing your apps, and only having your apps running full screen (i.e., filling the entire desktop) actually uses less power, as there's less for the graphics processor to draw, it not having to fill in all the fiddly bits with your desktop wallpaper etc.

Overall the power savings for your PC might seem small, but used correctly they can add up to significant savings over the course of a day, just as can quickly pressing the Power button on your tablet, or closing the lid of your laptop when you pop to the coffee machine, putting the PC to sleep.

"But!" you might say, "I use Microsoft Office all the time, that's a traditional desktop app, and not a store app." Well, Microsoft Office is available in the Microsoft Store and is downloadable from the Internet. Both versions are identical, with identical functionality. It just so happens that the Store version enables your PC to be more power-efficient.

▓ **Tip** Did you know that apps installed from the Microsoft Store are more secure than traditional desktop applications? This is because all store apps operate within their own "sandboxed" environment, and are protected from interacting with the operating system in the way traditional apps can. This means that if you only use Store apps, or use Windows 10 S, which can only install apps from the Store, your PC will be much more resistant to malware infection.

Finding and Understanding Settings

Throughout this book, I'll show you how to use different settings in Windows 10 to help you achieve more, and to make Windows 10 easier and more pleasant to use. It's probably good then to start with how you access and use those settings. You open the Settings app (or panel) by clicking the small *gear* icon in the Start menu, just above the Power button (see Figure 1-8).

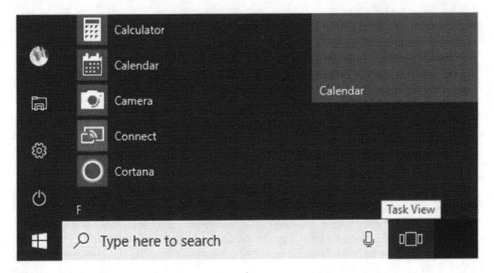

Figure 1-8. *Settings are accessed through the gear icon in the Start menu*

This opens the Settings app, which is organized into different categories, such as System, Devices, Network & Internet, and so on (see Figure 1-9). Above these category icons is a search box. You can type natural language search into this box to find what you're looking for and Windows 10 is extremely good at helping to find you the setting you need.

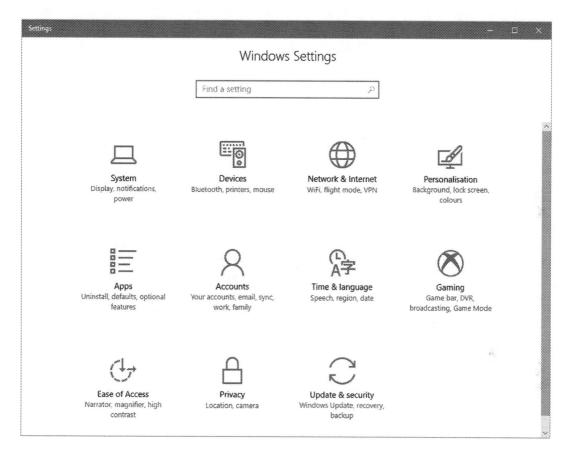

Figure 1-9. *The Settings app separates different settings into categories*

When you open a Settings category, you see that they are all laid out similarly with the subcategories of setting available to you in a list on the left side of the window, and the action settings for the currently selected subcategory on the right (see Figure 1-10).

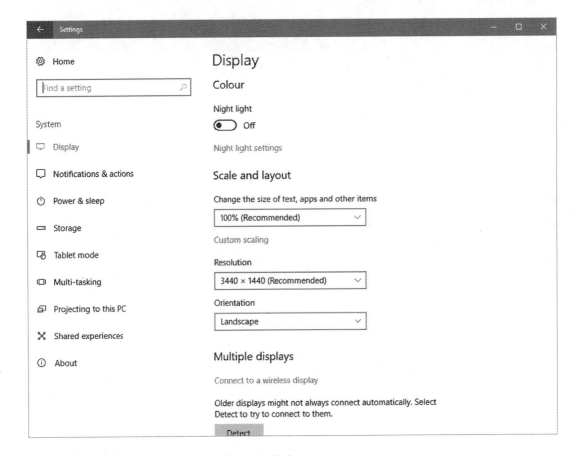

Figure 1-10. *Each Settings category is laid out similarly*

Within the different settings, you have the following options:

- A *switch* is a small rectangular button with rounded ends that is in either an *On* or an *Off* state.

- A *drop-down menu* is a rectangular box that you can click to choose from a list of options

- An *icon button* is highlighted in color and displays a shaded background or border when you hover your mouse or finger over it, indicating that you can click it to obtain further information or settings.

- *Links* are text displayed in a highlighted color to indicate you can click them for further information or more settings.

Summary

Microsoft has done a very good job of making Windows 10 easy to use and generally discoverable. If you've used any other version of Windows from XP onward, you'll find that what you want is generally where you expect to find it, and operates in the way that you would generally expect it to work.

Making Windows 10 work and operate as you want it to is a different matter. It's not just a matter of what you can do to harness its full power and potential, and how you can use its functions and features to become more productive. The first thing to do is to make it an environment in which you will enjoy working, which is something we'll look at in the next chapter.

CHAPTER 2

Making Your PC More Pleasurable to Use

You have no doubt changed the desktop wallpaper on your PC, probably many times. This means you know you can right-click in any blank space on the desktop to access the Personalization options. Did you know that's there's much more that you can do to make your desktop a more pleasurable space in which to work?

Personalizing the Lock Screen

Let's start with those Personalization options. They open the Settings app (or panel), which you can also open by clicking the "gear" icon on the bottom left of the Start menu. On the left, you see the main Settings categories. Clicking the Personalization icon displays the subcategory options for the Windows 10: Background, Colors, Lock screen, Themes, Start [menu] and taskbar (see Figure 2-1).

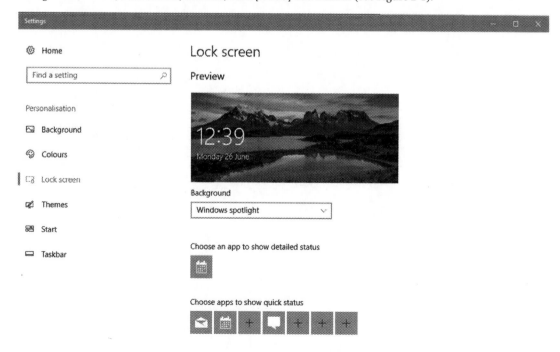

Figure 2-1. *You can personalize many aspects of the Windows desktop*

© Mike Halsey 2017
M. Halsey, *The Windows 10 Productivity Handbook*, https://doi.org/10.1007/978-1-4842-3294-1_2

The *lock screen* that you see before you sign in to your account on your PC is capable of displaying useful information. This includes counters for up to seven apps, such as your email and messenger, of how many (if any) notifications are waiting for you. In addition to this, you can have one app—perhaps your calendar—display more detailed information.

Making Windows 10 Easier on the Eye

Microsoft Windows has always been a very easy to customize operating system, and Windows 10 no exception. There are a variety of ways in which you can personalize the desktop experience, and make it a more fun place to be.

Changing the Desktop Wallpaper

The obvious place to begin with this—as it's the one thing most people seem to like to do—is to change the background wallpaper (sometimes called a *screensaver*, although a screensaver is a very different thing and no longer required in Windows 10).

In the Personalization ➤ Background Settings are easy and simple-to-use options for selecting a personalized desktop wallpaper. You can choose from one of the preselected wallpapers, or browse for a graphic or photograph on your PC.

If you find the wallpaper or photo doesn't fit properly on your screen, and you have black or colored bans to the left and right, or top and bottom of the image, click the *Choose a fit* drop-down menu. Here you can play safely with the various options (Fill, Fit, Stretch, Tile, Center, Span) until you get the wallpaper looking the way you want it to.

Changing Colors

If you prefer adding a little more color to your desktop, there are a couple of ways you can do it. In Personalization ➤ Colors you can choose from a variety of accent colors for your desktop, Start menu, taskbar, and apps. It's worth scrolling down to the bottom of the Colors settings. Here you find additional options, such as turning on transparency effects, which mostly affect the Start menu and Action Center, but that can also make some apps much more pleasurable to use, and you can choose to show or hide the accent color on the Start menu, taskbar, Action Center, and the title bars of open apps (see Figure 2-2).

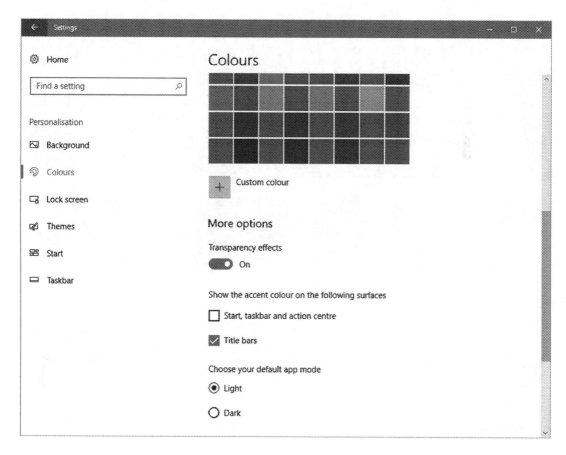

Figure 2-2. *You can choose how color affects your desktop and apps*

Furthermore, if that's not enough for you, you can customize Windows 10 with Themes, and you'll find the link to these in the Personalization settings panel. You can customize different aspects of the desktop environment, such as sounds, colors, and your mouse cursor, or you can download themes from the Microsoft Store (see Figure 2-3). There are hundreds, probably thousands by the time you read this, of these themes, all of which can help you customize your desktop to look and feel the way you would like it to.

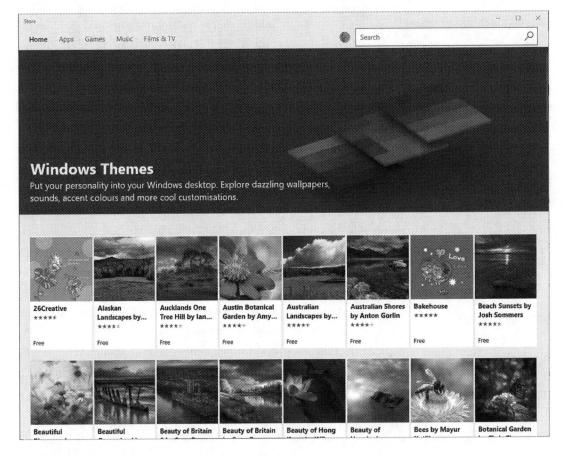

Figure 2-3. *You can customize Windows 10 with themes*

Right-clicking in a blank space on the desktop, and then clicking the *Display settings* link on the context menu that appears, enables you to activate the *Night Light* feature I mentioned earlier, where each evening you can have the color temperature of the PC change, causing less strain on your eyes and ultimately making it easier for you to sleep afterward.

Making Text and On-Screen Items Easier to Read and Use

If you find text small and difficult to read on your screen, adjusting the Text Scaling option can make it much easier to see and read (see Figure 2-4). Also, if you work with multiple monitors (many people do), this is where you'll find all the controls that you need. You can determine things such as which icons appear on what taskbar, and on which screens the taskbar appears.

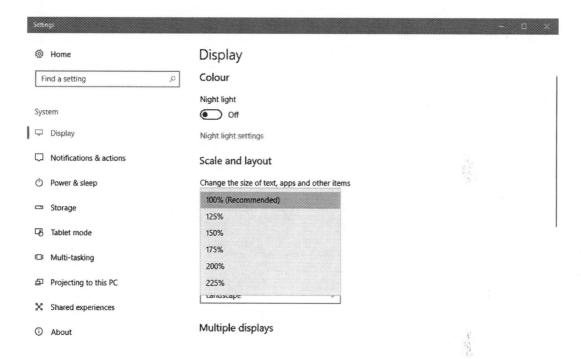

Figure 2-4. *You can change the scaling and size of text*

Additional categories on the left side of the panel, allow you to easily configure Notifications, the Action Center, when the PC goes to sleep, the way that Tablet mode operates, and more.

People tend to think the purpose of the Accessibility features in Windows is to help people who have cognitive, physical, visual, or auditory needs. What would you say if I told you that there are features in the Windows' Ease of Access settings that can make PCs easier to use for many people—perhaps even you. If you want to know more about making Windows 10 easier to use, my book, *Windows 10 Accessibility Handbook* (Apress, 2015), is available to buy at http://pcs.tv/2xwy2oo and from all good booksellers.

Alongside the Narrator, Magnifier, and High Contrast options are some that are more generally useful. The *Keyboard* options for example (see Figure 2-5), contain the ability to make two and three key combinations, such as Ctrl+C (Copy), Ctrl+V (Paste) and Ctrl+Alt+Del easier to use by allowing you to only press one key at a time.

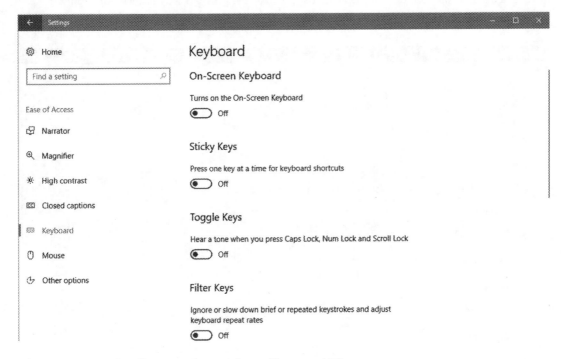

Figure 2-5. Many Ease of Access options can be used by general PC users

The feature that can sound a tone when you press the Caps Lock, Number Lock, or Scroll Lock keys can be more useful still. Imagine how helpful it would have been to hear a beep every time you accidentally pressed Caps Lock when you didn't intend to.

You can also use the Filter Keys option to ignore, or slow down the repeated keystrokes that can occur if you hold a key down for just a little too long.

In the *Other options* controls (see Figure 2-6), you can choose to disable desktop and window animations, which some people can find distracting, or to hide the desktop wallpaper altogether.

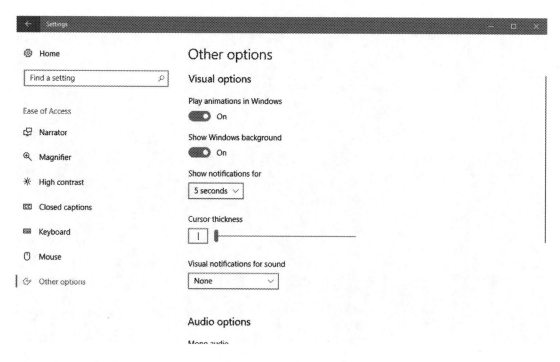

Figure 2-6. *Additional Ease of Access options can help almost anybody*

A Notification option also allows you to change the default time popup notifications appear from 5 seconds to 5 minutes, perhaps making them easier to read, especially if you have to pop away from the PC a lot, or if find them distracting, for which there is also the *Quiet Hours* feature.

If you, like many people, sometimes find the mouse cursor in your documents difficult to find, you can make it larger. You can also choose a visual notification, such as flashing the current window when an alert or notification is received, useful if you work in a noisy environment, such as a factory or call center.

Features that can make your PC easier to use aren't just limited to the Ease of Access panel. The Night Light feature that I mentioned earlier, which changes the color temperature of the screen, making it more yellow in appearance, can sometimes help people with dyslexia to read what's on the screen more easily.

What's more, enabling Tablet mode all the time spaces out icons, and makes some icons larger, so they are easier to find and click. This happens in both the desktop environment and in many apps as well.

If you want something different for your desktop, and for apps and Windows features, you can enable *Dark* mode in the Colors settings of the Personalization options (see Figure 2-7).

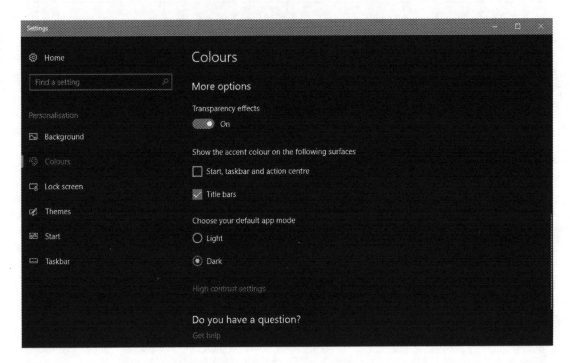

Figure 2-7. You can switch between light and dark windows themes

You might find that the Dark theme makes the PC easier to use, or you may just prefer it. Note here that apps have their own settings for a Dark theme (if they support it). Look for the Settings icon (the cog) within the app itself.

Lastly, and again in the Color settings, there is the option to use or disable the Transparency effects in Windows 10. Some people find these effects a distraction, but they can quickly be switched off if you wish.

Changing Region Settings for the PC

PCs are used all across the world, and people work right around the world. You might be an American working in the Middle East, or a South Korean in the heart of Europe. Either way, unless you're using the laptop or the tablet that you brought with you, you'll find yourself faced with local language, date, and number settings for the country you find yourself in.

The *Date & time* settings can be used to adjust these features in the operating system to better suit your own needs (see Figure 2-8).

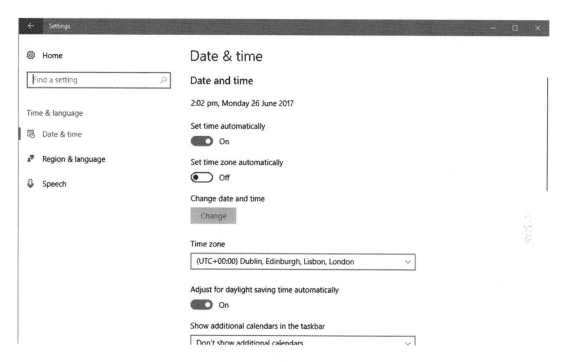

Figure 2-8. *You can adjust regional settings for your PC*

It's also in the *Date & time* settings that you can change your current location and time zone, and add or remove additional language packs on the PC.

▩ **Tip**   In the modern Internet age, we all value what little privacy we still have. Companies and scammers are always trying to obtain data about us, and this does include Microsoft. The *Privacy* settings let you take overall control of this, however. You can switch off almost everything, Microsoft still need some very basic metrics so that Windows Update can work, but this does include switching off information that is collected by, or passed to advertisers, through apps.

The *Location* settings can also help protect your privacy if you do not use apps on your PC, such as mapping, that need to know where you are. Lastly, the *Camera* and *Microphone* settings prevent apps from recording unless you specifically want them to.

That Syncing Feeling

So you've set up and personalized your PC the way you want it. But now you have to go and do it all over again on your other Windows 10 PCs and devices, right? Actually, no, but only if you signed in to the PC using a Microsoft account. Opening *Accounts* in the Settings panel, and then clicking *Sync your settings* allows you to synchronize your settings, themes, passwords, browser favorites, language settings, and wallpaper across to all the other PCs on which you also sign in using the same Microsoft account (see Figure 2-9).

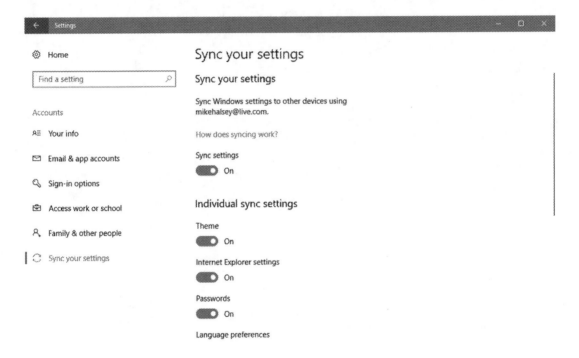

Figure 2-9. *You can sync settings across your Windows 10 PCs and devices*

Syncing your settings like this can be an enormous time saver, especially when it comes to saving an Internet bookmark on one PC, and then wanting access to it on another.

It's worth noting that a company or organization may sync your settings and preferences automatically on their server, thus not requiring you to have a Microsoft account to sign in to the PC, or they may block this functionality for security reasons.

Summary

In this chapter, I've only just scratched the surface of what you can do to customize your desktop and app experience, to make working on your PC more pleasurable. I encourage you to play around with the customization options you find either when you right-click the desktop, taskbar, or in the Start menu, or that can be found in the Settings panel (by clicking the cog icon in the bottom-left corner of the Start menu).

In the next chapter, we'll look at some of the productivity-focused features of Windows 10, such as the Cortana digital assistant, how you can work with and manage multiple windows and apps on your desktop simultaneously, and how you can use pen and ink support to its best effect.

CHAPTER 3

Achieving More with Windows 10

It's clear that there's much that you can configure in Windows 10. There are many features that you can utilize that can make your working environment more pleasant. And we all know that a pleasant working environment is one in which most people do their best work.

It doesn't end there, though. What I detailed in Chapters 1 and 2 can be considered the "low-end" features and enhancements. There's much more that Windows 10 can do to make your working life easier, simpler, and more productive.

Cortana: Much More Than a Personal Assistant

People can tend to think of digital personal assistants, such as Siri and Cortana, as that thing you're embarrassed to talk to on your smartphone while you sit in a café. While this is largely true, and I don't like to be seen talking to my phone in public any more than the next person, Cortana is actually much more than this.

If you click the Cortana icon on your taskbar, you are shown that you can ask Cortana to perform acts, such as changing the time of your afternoon appointment, finding the value of a stock price or showing you what films are playing nearby. All of these are useful, but are geared around speaking to Cortana. Clicking the Notebook icon on the left of the Cortana window details a full range of ways in which Cortana can be customized, and information about things she can do (see Figure 3-1).

© Mike Halsey 2017

M. Halsey, *The Windows 10 Productivity Handbook*, https://doi.org/10.1007/978-1-4842-3294-1_3

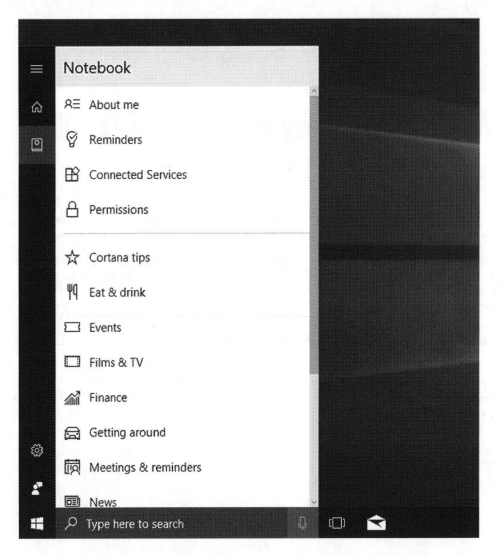

Figure 3-1. *Cortana is highly configurable*

Cortana can be programmed with your home and work locations in the *About me* settings (you can also set these locations in the Windows 10 Maps app). Doing so can allow Cortana to provide you with information about traffic and transport issues, and allow her (I hate calling Cortana an "it") to offer help and support based on where you are, thus doing so more intelligently.

Intelligent Reminders

Allowing Cortana access to your email, calendar, and messaging history (primarily through Skype or Microsoft Teams) can allow her to offer support and reminders based on what's going on, and who contacts you.

If, for example, someone contacts you to suggest a meeting at 3pm on Friday, and you have an appointment at the dentist at that time, Cortana can give you a gentle nudge, allowing you to suggest an alternative time or day.

As another example, if you emailed the boss (assuming you're not already the boss) saying that you'd have the quarterly sales report for them by Wednesday afternoon, Cortana offers to set a reminder for the event, so you don't forget.

Reminders can also be location-based, meaning you can set a reminder to buy flowers for your partner when you're next in the city center, put the trash out when you get home, or call Tricia when you arrive in Vancouver.

For other people who use Cortana, you can set reminders based on their own proximity, such as reminding you to tell Phil about the special offer on the hotel he wanted to book when you're next with him. Cortana knows when you're both in the same place, and pops up a nudge.

Cortana can even integrate with the Windows 10 desktop *Sticky Notes*, offering to help when you type something, such as a web address, date, or phone number.

What's perhaps more useful, and less intrusive in the eyes of some people, is that Cortana can scan your email for information, such as deliveries and flights. It can then automatically create calendar events and optional reminders for them, and assist you with parcel and flight tracking.

Connected to Everything

Cortana isn't just about what's happening on your PC, and your email. It can be connected to other devices and services. For example, if you set a reminder or alert on your PC, but you're not at that PC when the time comes, the alert will be triggered on the device you're using. This could be your laptop, tablet, or smartphone (Cortana is supported on both iOS and Android, so look for the Cortana app in the store).

You can connect Cortana to your Office 365 account, Dynamics CRM system, LinkedIn, and more through the *Connected Accounts* settings. Additionally, Windows Store apps can plug themselves into Cortana, enabling you to more easily control them. There are many apps that support this functionality, including Uber, Netflix, and Fitbit.

Then There's Everything Else

Naturally, Cortana can tell you about the weather, offer recipe advice, and tell you about nearby restaurants, just as you can with other personal digital assistants. She can also allow you dictate, and easily send and respond to different types of message including SMS, email, and instant messages (where they're supported by the message service's app). Cortana can also connect to your Internet of Things (IoT) devices, such as lighting, security system, and so forth.

Microsoft is expanding the features and functionality of Cortana all the time, so it's worth checking her out occasionally to see if any new options have appeared. In the meantime, and in your quiet moments of downtime, try asking her to tell you a joke, sing you a song, or even speak Klingon.

Windows Ink

Two-in-One hybrid devices, such as the Microsoft Surface Pro, are becoming more and more popular, especially in the boardroom, as they allow you to have a device with a pen on which you can scribble notes, and work in a way that can (for some people at least) be more natural than using a keyboard and trackpad or mouse.

Naturally, for a company that makes professional-grade touchscreen PCs, the Windows Ink system is well-thought-out and integrated into many aspects of the operating system and its apps.

In the system tray to the right of the desktop taskbar, there is an icon on touchscreen devices for the *Windows Ink Workspace*. This pop-out panel includes quick links to some of the things that you can do with your pen or stylus (see Figure 3-2). Note that if you don't see the Windows Ink Workspace icon, right-click the taskbar, and click the Show Windows Ink Workspace option.

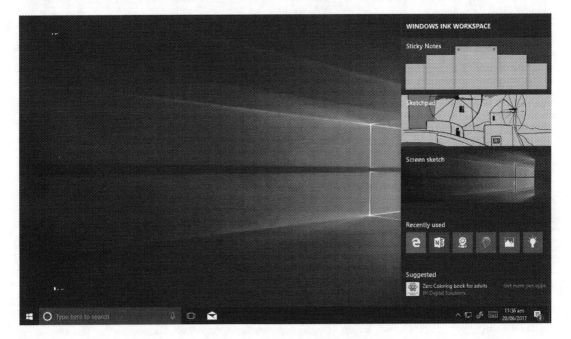

Figure 3-2. *The Windows Ink workspace can be triggered from the system tray*

In addition to writing in Sticky Notes, or using the Sketchboard or Whiteboard apps, or annotating notes in OneNote, you can draw on and annotate your PC's screen and send a screenshot to a friend or colleague.

The Microsoft Edge web browser, which comes with Windows 10, has a pen annotation icon to the right of the address bar. This allows you to annotate, highlight, snip, and share web pages easily (see Figure 3-3).

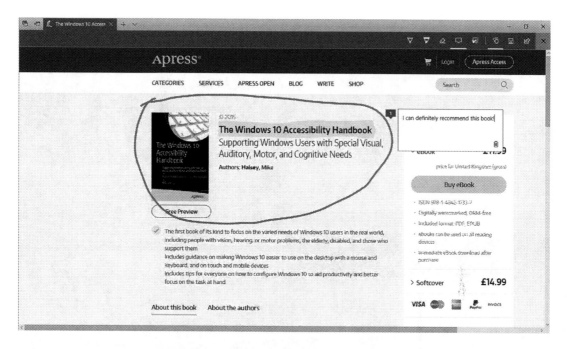

Figure 3-3. *You can annotate web pages in the Edge browser*

There's plenty more you can do in the Edge browser as well, including highlighting some text and then right-clicking it (a touch and hold works as well), or right clicking an image and asking Cortana to give you more information about it.

▓ **Tip**   If you need to access international characters on your PC, but you don't want to open the Character Map utility, or try to remember the keyboard shortcuts for them, open the on-screen keyboard from the system tray. Then, when you touch and hold any letter, all the international characters and symbols related to that letter appear in a pop-up window from which you can select them.

Snap!

How many windows do you have open on your desktop at any one time? One? Two? Four? Eight? More? In the past, managing our desktop workspace was solved by using a multi-monitor setup of two or three screens; and more recently, by purchasing a monitor with a higher resolution, such as 4K or even 5K. I use a 21:9 aspect ratio curved ultrawide monitor (primarily for playing *Elite: Dangerous*) and I can thoroughly recommend them if for no other reason than spreadsheets look amazing (Easy now, Ed.). In Windows 10, however, none of this is actually necessary, as you can manage your windows and apps on any type and size of screen.

Snap is a feature that works with any windows on your desktop, even ones you have minimized. You can drag any window to the left, the right, or any of the four corners of the screen, and a glass-effect outline shows you that the windows are snapped there when you release it. This means you can snap two or even four different windows simultaneously, making them easier to see and access.

Additionally, when you snap a window, if you have other apps open on your desktop (including minimized apps), you are presented with a thumbnail view of those apps (see Figure 3-4). Clicking or tapping one causes it to automatically expand to fill the remaining space on your screen.

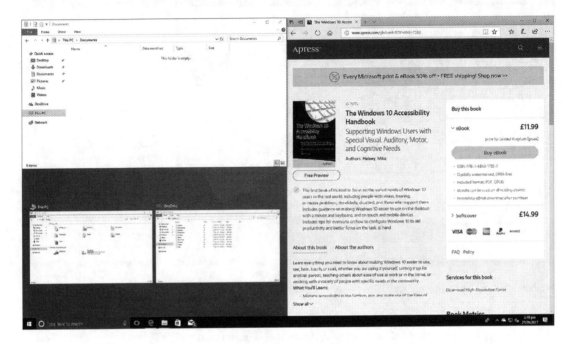

Figure 3-4. *Snap is an effective way to manage your apps*

When you have the windows snapped on your screen, they can be dynamically resized, with windows taking all of the strain out of the process. If you move your mouse to the join between two apps, a black bar appears. You can drag this bar to resize one app, with the other snapped app automatically expanding or contracting to fill the remainder of the space (see Figure 3-5). This can be very useful if you are working on a document while referring to reference material, as an example.

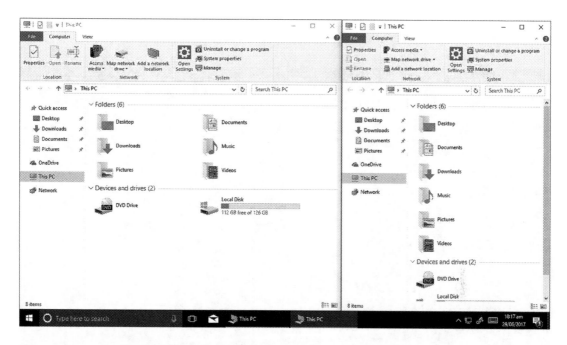

Figure 3-5. *You can dynamically resize snapped windows*

It's worth pointing out, as you might be wondering, that when you unsnap any app, by dragging it away from the edge of the screen, it always returns to the same size and shape it was before you snapped it.

▦ **Tip**   You can control snap through some quick keyboard shortcuts. Use the Windows key + the Left arrow or the Right arrow to snap the currently selected window to the left or right of the screen. To move the snapped window to the top or bottom corner, use the Windows key + the Up or Down arrow keys.

Additionally, you can use the Windows key + the Up or Down arrow keys to maximize, minimize, or restore the currently selected window.

Working with Virtual Desktops

The *Task View* virtual desktop feature in Windows 10 is something that I'm fond of calling "boss mode," because, let's be honest, it's a good way to play Candy Crush or shop on eBay, and be able to instantly switch back to a desktop with only your customer relations manager or accounting software when your boss comes into the room.

Think of it as the feature that Simon Pegg's character, Benji Dunn, uses when he's playing Halo on his office PC in *Mission: Impossible 5*; he's instantly able to switch back to his CIA analytics software when someone approaches. This is something that I'm certain happens every day in the real world.

Now I'm not encouraging you to sneak an Xbox controller into the office, or to spend the day looking at garden furniture, but I'm sure you take my point about how the Task View feature can be used to create separate and distinct working environments on your PC.

Task View is activated from the icon on the taskbar that looks like three small rectangles, and it allows you to create, close, and manage "virtual" desktops (see Figure 3-6).

Figure 3-6. *Task View can be used to configure multiple desktops*

When you create a new desktop, you can use the Task View button to switch between it and any other desktops that you have created; the icon to create a new desktop sits near the bottom right of your screen, and the desktops appear as live thumbnails in the bottom center.

This means that you can organize your open apps so that they're not all running in the same space. You might want, for example, an Excel spreadsheet full screen on one desktop, while keeping Microsoft Teams and Outlook separate on another desktop.

You can control Task View directly from keyboard shortcuts as well. Windows key + Ctrl + D will create a new virtual desktop and switch to it, and the Windows key + Ctrl + F4 will close the current virtual desktop. You can also use the Windows key + Ctrl + the left and right arrow keys to switch (left and right) between virtual desktops.

While there is no keyboard shortcut to move an app from one virtual desktop to another, you can achieve this by opening the Task View... view, and right-clicking the app that you want to move. A context menu then appears, in which you see a *Move to* option (see Figure 3-7).

Figure 3-7. *You can move apps between virtual desktops*

You will notice in this context menu are options to *Show this window on all desktops* and to *Show windows from this app on all desktops*. These options might prove useful to you.

Additionally, in the Task View... view, if you mouse over one of the virtual desktop thumbnails a close icon will appear. If you close a virtual desktop that has open apps on it, those apps **won't** be closed. Instead, they'll be moved to an adjacent desktop.

Pick Up Where You Left Off with Timeline

There are many advantages to using Windows Store apps in Windows 10 over the more traditional win32 desktop apps. For starters, they're easier to install and update. They don't use as much battery power on your laptop, tablet, or 2-in-1 device because there's no system tray updater to run in the background, and because the app is suspended when it's not the one in use in the foreground on your desktop. Additionally, they include functionality that win32 apps simply can't provide.

A feature that isn't in Windows 10 at the time of writing, but it is well worth mentioning because it could be in the operating system by the time you read this (it is definitely coming), is the ability to begin work in an app on one device and continue it later on a different device from exactly the point where you left it. This feature uses the cloud, your company network, or a Bluetooth connection to enable your different Windows 10 apps to "talk" to each other, transferring details of your currently open file(s) and their status when you stop working on one device, and move to another, where Cortana asks you if you want to pick up where you left off.

Timeline works on Windows 10, Cortana-enabled iOS, and Android devices to help you work seamlessly across all the devices you use. Imagine, closing your laptop lid when you're half way through a creating a presentation, then picking up that work on your desktop back in the office the moment you get there. Or having some browser tabs open on your smartphone, with your web browser on your desktop PC automatically opening those same tabs for you when you use it.

Timeline is strictly an opt-in feature, and it needs to be actively built-into Windows Store apps to work. When it is released, it will be included with the Windows Store versions of Microsoft Office and may well be built into the next version of Office 365, coming in mid- to late 2018. Options will be available in the app's settings if the app supports this feature. You will be able to find out more about, and control Timeline by searching for it in the Settings app or in Cortana.

Managing Printers in Windows 10

I was still at school when technologists first began talking about the "paperless office." The idea being that we'd be able to do everything digitally on our computers, and there would be no need for printing in offices, homes, and workplaces any more.

Sadly, the truth is very different as we're still printing every bit as much as we used to. Sometimes, this is because we simply don't trust that we'll be able to present or read a digital copy of a document; sometimes, it's because we know we'll have to scrawl all over it; sometimes, we need to read it on the train on the way home or on the way to a meeting; and sometimes, it's because the businesses or organizations we work with just haven't moved their systems to digitized structures yet.

There's still a lot that we do almost entirely electronically, as your local post office will testify with a grumble, but you won't find a home or business anywhere that doesn't still have at least one printer in regular use.

Managing those printers can be a pain, especially as the majority of PCs these days are mobile devices, such as laptops, 2-in-1 hybrids, or tablets. It's just annoying sending something to a printer to discover it's the wrong printer you sent it to, and nothing has appeared in the paper tray.

In the settings app, under *Devices* ➤ *Printers & scanners*, is the list of printers that are installed on the PC. You can click the *Manage* button to view its print queue, remove its driver, or set it as the default printer. Below the list of printers is a check box that you might find useful.

Let Windows manage my default printer (see Figure 3-8) allows Windows 10 to change the default printer based on the location you find yourself in. Note that you'll need to have *Location services* enabled in the privacy options for this work, but it can help make sure you get more accurate default printers so that when you're at home, or in the office, anything you send to be printed will automatically go to the correct printer.

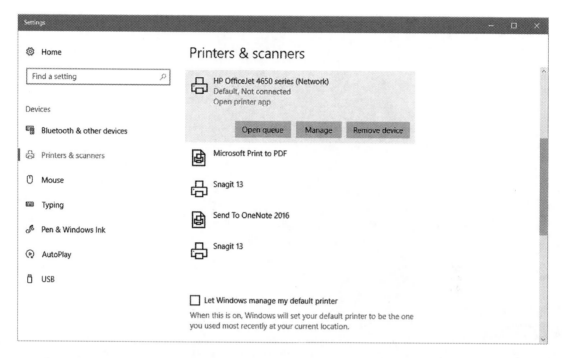

Figure 3-8. *You can set default printers for different locations*

This feature works by tying the default printer to the network you're connected to at the time. Whenever you switch to using another of your known networks, Windows automatically detects that you used a different printer last time you were connected, and make the default printer change for you.

Using OneDrive Files On-Demand

One of the biggest issues facing mobile workers is a lack of available storage space for your files and documents. My own laptop comes with a 512GB solid state disk (SSD), of which Windows 10 and my apps occupies about 20% of it, but my entire stored library of documents, photos, music, and video that's backed up in the cloud is almost 1TB, double the capacity of the laptop when the SSD is empty.

When you connect to OneDrive or OneDrive for Business, you can choose what files from the cloud are also stored on your PC. Each file that's backed up to OneDrive has an icon overlaid on its thumbnail image in File Explorer. These icons (see Figure 3-9), signify if the file is located in the cloud only, in the cloud and on your PC, or if it's just in the cloud but currently being downloaded and synced.

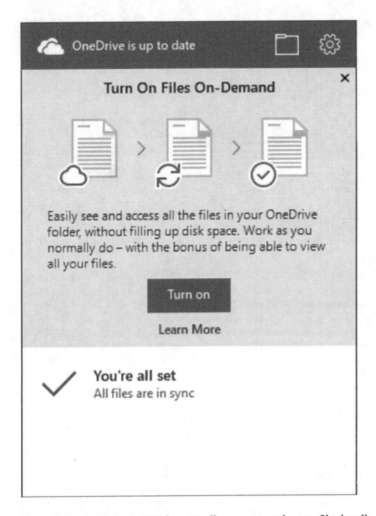

Figure 3-9. *OneDrive in Windows 10 allows you to only store files locally as you need them*

The upshot of Files On-Demand is that you are always able to see thumbnail images of *all* the files and documents that you have stored on OneDrive or OneDrive for Business on your PC; they are only downloaded and stored locally if you specify this in the OneDrive Settings (right-click the cloud icon in the system tray) or when you open a downloaded file, it is thereafter stored locally on the PC.

Using OneDrive File Versioning

Another useful feature that's coming to Windows 10 in the near future, but that's not available as I write this, is File Versioning using OneDrive. Sometimes you'll be working on a file and make changes that you didn't intend to make, or you'll delete a file that you didn't intend to delete. It happens, especially if like me, you're fond of pressing Ctrl+S (Save) regularly, or using Shift+Del to bypass the recycle bin when deleting files.

OneDrive's file versioning tool allows you to recover previous versions of files on your PC in two ways. The first is by right-clicking a file, which presents the *Restore Previous Versions* option. Clicking this option presents a list of all the backed up versions of the file that exist in the cloud (you don't need to have them backed up locally) from which you can choose one to restore.

It's not yet known how File Versioning will work, or exactly what the feature will end up being called, but it's worth looking out for when major updates to Windows 10 are delivered to your PCs.

Summary

There are so many cool and great ways to achieve more with Windows 10; some of which are so cool that they're worth mentioning here, even though they've been officially announced, they won't appear in Windows 10 until sometime late in 2018. Cortana on her own is an incredibly powerful, flexible, and useful assistant. It's well worth playing around with Cortana to see what she can do, and check in with her when there's a major update to Windows 10 to see what's been added.

While there's much you can do with Windows 10 to boost your productivity that's not the end of it by any stretch. There are a whole host of tips and tricks you can use to get even more productivity benefit from your PCs and Windows 10 devices, and in the next chapter that's what I'll show you.

CHAPTER 4

Productivity Boost Tips and Tricks

I don't think there's any doubt so far that there are a huge number of features included in Windows 10 that you can use to help boost your productivity and the enjoyment of using your PCs and devices. It doesn't end there because there are a wide variety of smaller tools and features that can also help make your workday more pleasurable.

Shake It All About!

How many windows do you have open on your desktop at any one time? It's very common for people to having as many as ten or more windows open. When you need to concentrate on one specific app or task, though, this clutter can make it difficult to concentrate.

A quick workaround is to grab the top of the window that you need to concentrate on, and give it a good shake. This causes all the other windows on your desktop to minimize. Don't worry, when you want those windows back, shake the app again and they'll all reappear just as they were before.

Tip   Sometimes shaking the mouse can be annoying, especially if you have motor or reflex problems, or if you just find it difficult using a mouse. The ability to disable *shake* has not been built into the Settings panel at the time of writing (although it may be worth searching for it in the future in the *Ease of Access* ➤ *Mouse* options).

Search in the Start menu for the Control Panel. From there open the Ease of Access Center, and then click *Make the mouse easier to use*. You see a check box that enables you to *Prevent windows from being automatically arranged when moved to the edge of the screen*. This disables shake, but bear in mind that it also disables the snap feature.

Taking a Quick Peek

While we're on the subject of having many apps and windows open at once, you may also have many running apps minimized to the taskbar. If you want to check an app, hover your mouse over its taskbar icon— a thumbnail image of the app will pop up (see Figure 4-1). If you then move your mouse over the thumbnail image, the full app will appear on your desktop, and all the other windows are temporarily hidden.

© Mike Halsey 2017

M. Halsey, *The Windows 10 Productivity Handbook*, https://doi.org/10.1007/978-1-4842-3294-1_4

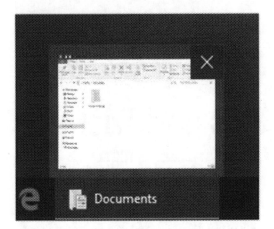

Figure 4-1. *You can peek at previews of minimized apps*

■ **Tip**   In previous versions of Windows, you might remember that you could click the far right edge of the taskbar to make all of your windows become transparent, so you could see any widgets of sticky notes that you have placed on the desktop. This feature still exists in Windows 10, although it is disabled in some versions.

To activate it, right-click the taskbar and from the menu that appears, open the settings. Here you can disable or enable the options to *Use peek to preview the desktop when you move your mouse* to the *Show desktop button at the end of the taskbar.*

Keeping Things Quiet

Nothing is more annoying than pop-up alerts and messages bugging you when you're trying to concentrate; although as I'm writing this (as it often happens when I write), there's some quiet Jean-Michel Jarre playing in the background.

Windows 10 offers a feature called *Quiet hours,* which is activated from the quick actions buttons in the *Action Center* (see Figure 4-2). Clicking the *Quiet hours* button automatically silences all notifications and pop-up alerts.

Figure 4-2. *You can enable quiet hours in Windows 10*

Additionally, you can configure what apps are allowed to display pop-up alerts and notifications, and disable those you don't want to see. You can do this in the Settings panel, by clicking *System ➤ Notifications & actions*, where you see a list of apps that can display notifications; each has an on/off switch (see Figure 4-3).

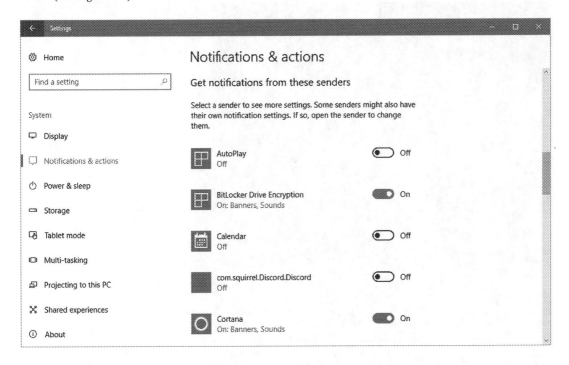

Figure 4-3. *You can manage what apps display alerts and pop-up menus*

It's well worth spending a little time configuring what apps are, and are not allowed to pester you with alerts. As an example, you're probably going to check your social media and messaging feeds several times a day, so do you really need them to alert you immediately upon receipt of a message or other notification, or can these wait for a short while so you can press on with something else? It's all a matter of personal preferences and priorities, and it's worth considering when configuring notifications and alerts.

Manage Your Quick Actions Buttons

While we're on the subject, you can customize your quick actions buttons by opening the Settings panel and clicking *System ➤ Notifications & actions*, where you will see an option to *Add or remove quick actions*. The panel allows you to drag-and-drop quick actions icons onto its 4×4 grid, so you can have the buttons that you use and need the most where you want them to be (see Figure 4-4).

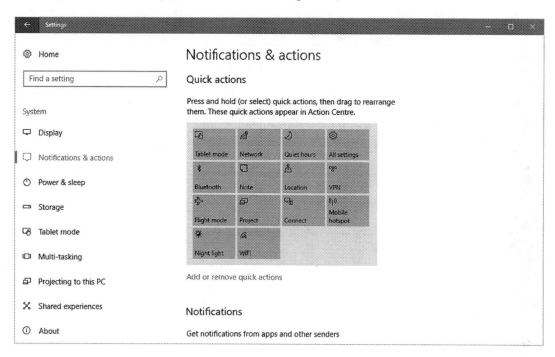

Figure 4-4. *You can customize your quick actions buttons*

One thing to bear in mind when configuring your quick actions buttons is that if you are using a laptop or tablet, and you travel frequently, it might be worth putting *Airplane mode* (Flight mode in some countries) near the top of the list. Conversely, on a desktop, you can deprecate this and perhaps other buttons, such as *Tablet mode* and *Mobile hotspot*, if you see them in the list.

Smart Search

We all need to search our PCs for files and documents, and search online for—well, just about everything. I'll cover search in much more depth in Chapter 3, but to summarize here, Cortana has some clever search functionality built-in that can help you define the parameters of your search effectively. When you begin typing in Cortana, you see some icons and a *Filters* option appear at the top of the search results window (see Figure 4-5).

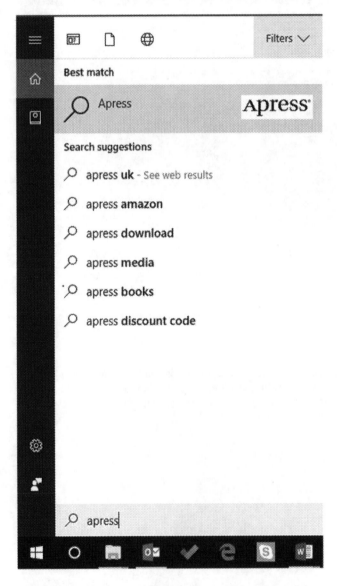

Figure 4-5. *Cortana provides filters for searching files and documents on your PC*

The Icons allow you to specify your search is for installed apps on the PC, documents, or if you want to search online. Additionally the filters allow you to specify what type of document to search for, such as videos or music. Below these options in the Filters section is a button to *Change where Windows searches*. You can use this option to add (or remove) search locations, which can be especially useful if you are storing documents on a disk that is not automatically indexed by Windows.

File Explorer also includes a search box (near its upper-right corner). If you click here, a search tab opens on the ribbon, where you have some advanced searching options (see Figure 4-6).

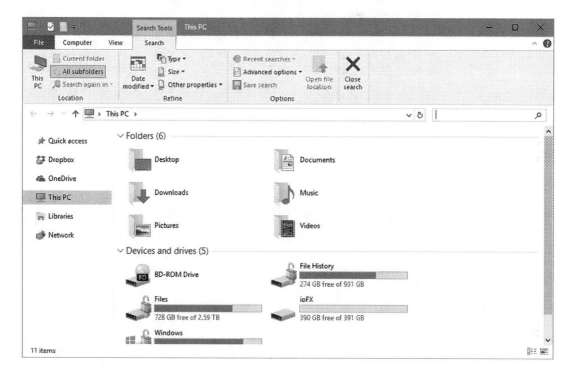

Figure 4-6. *File Explorer contains advanced search options*

You can choose from the options available, such as date modified or kind, or you can type a search command directly into the search box. This is called *Advanced Query Syntax* and I have included a full list of all the search commands available in Windows 10 in Appendix D at the end of this book.

At first, this might seem complex, but Windows 10 helps you with your search; for example, if you type Kind: in the search box to search for a specific type of file, you get a drop-down menu with valid options from which you can choose. This context menu changes according to the search term that you type (see Figure 4-7). Search in Windows 10 is covered in more depth in Chapter 3.

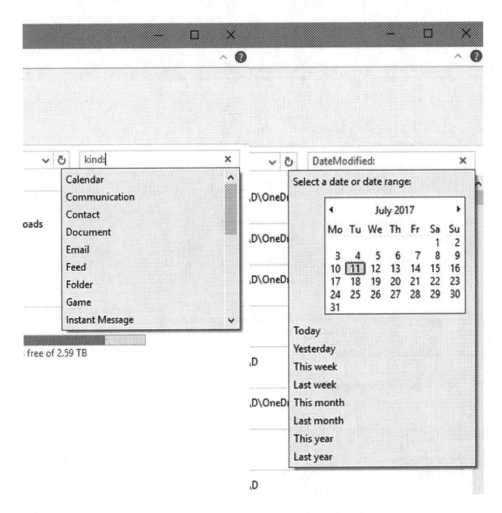

Figure 4-7. *You can use Advanced Query Syntax to search your PC*

▓ **Tip**   If you regularly search for the same thing in File Explorer, you can click the *Save search* button to save that search so you can use it again (see Figure 4-8). This saves the search to your [Username] ➤ Searches folder, although you can choose to save it to another location if you wish, such as your desktop. Every time you run the search, it automatically and dynamically updates to include and reflect any new and changed files and documents that are relevant.

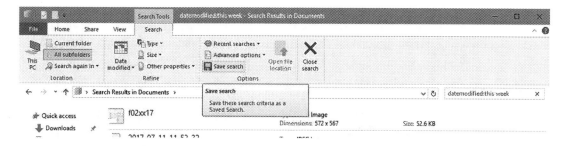

Figure 4-8. *You can save searches in Windows 10*

Managing Battery Life and Background Apps

In Chapter 1, I detailed some of my top tips for maximizing the battery life on your laptop or tablet, but there are also finer and more granular controls available. Open the Settings panel and click *System* ➤ *Power & sleep.* You'll be faced with the options to change when the screen turns off and when the PC goes to sleep.

The *Additional power settings* link opens more options. Here you can choose the action of the Power button, such as enable and disable features like Sleep and Hibernate (see Figure 4-9).

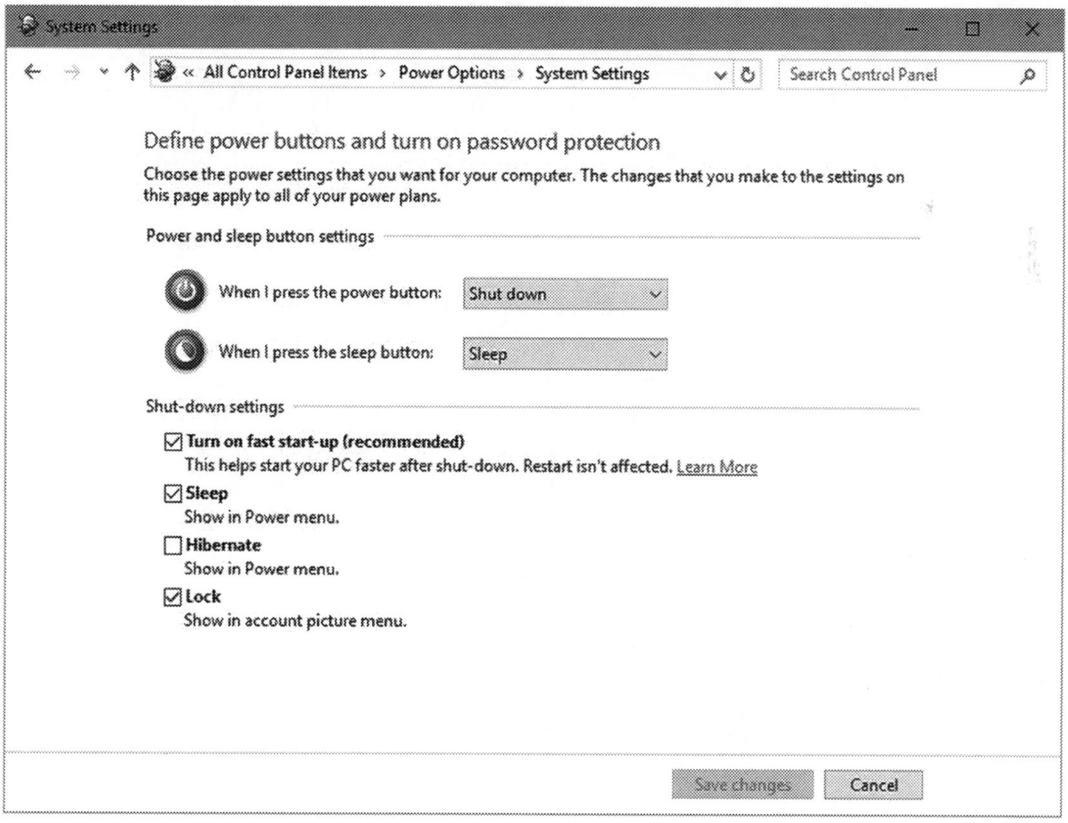

Figure 4-9. *You can change additional power settings*

> ▒ **Note** What is the difference between Sleep and Hibernate? Sleep keeps the memory of the PC intact, so you can start working again extremely quickly when you return to your PC. This does use power, however, so the Hibernate option writes the contents of the PC's memory to the hard disk, enabling it to stop using power. Once a PC has been in sleep mode for the few hours it automatically hibernates to save the battery.

Additionally you can create power plans for the PC, so you can more easily control the power usage of the PC. Doing so also allows you to *Change advanced power settings* in which there are options to control when devices such as your hard disk or USB devices are powered down.

Using the Mobility Center

On a laptop or tablet, the Mobility Center, which is most easily accessed from the pop-up menu that appears when you press the Windows key + X, is a great place from which to control your display brightness, volume, battery options, and screen rotation. It's also where you activate Presentation mode (see Figure 4-10).

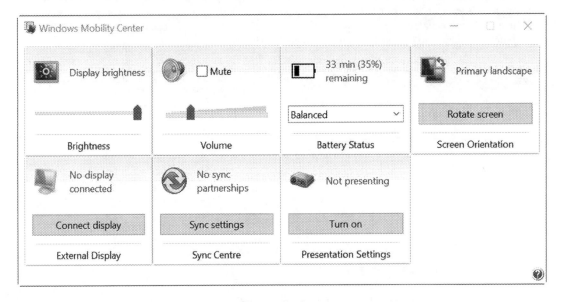

Figure 4-10. *Windows Mobility Center offers useful functionality*

Presentation mode silences pop-up alerts and notifications (as the *Quiet hours* feature does), but it also prevents the screen from turning off or the PC going to sleep or into hibernation when you are using it during presentations.

Summary

Clearly, there are a multitude of features and utilities in Windows 10 that you can use to enhance your productivity and to make the desktop a more pleasant environment in which to work.

We're still not done, though, because in the next chapter, we'll look at how you can maximize your Windows experience. In Chapter 6, we'll examine how you can search for files, documents, folders, messages, and people online. I'll bring together what we've covered so far, and look at how we can organize our desktops and PCs to create an optimal working environment.

CHAPTER 5

Maximize Your Windows Experience

So far in this book, I've shown you a whole raft of features and utilities that you can use to help you become more productive when using your PC, and to help you enjoy the experience more. Individually they can perhaps seem quite complex and daunting, so I want to spend some time looking at how all of this fits together, so you can create a cohesive working experience, and how you can use some of the more useful features in more depth.

Getting Your Day Started

Your day starts at the lock screen (see Figure 5-1). Bleary-eyed you'll stare at it for a few seconds before dismissing it, and signing in to start another dreary day. Well, this might be exaggerating the point somewhat but I'm sure you know what I mean. The lock screen is just an artificial barrier between you and your working environment.

© Mike Halsey 2017
M. Halsey, *The Windows 10 Productivity Handbook*, https://doi.org/10.1007/978-1-4842-3294-1_5

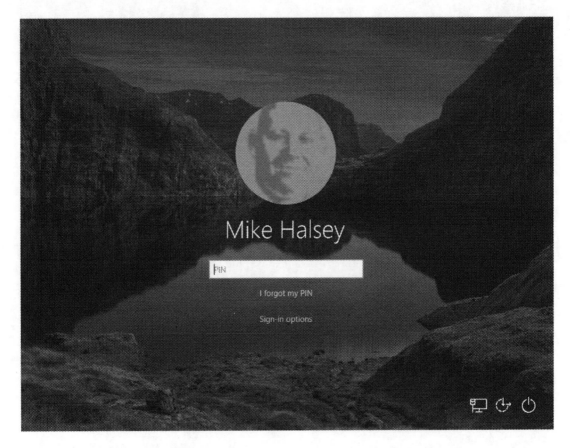

Figure 5-1. *The Windows 10 lock screen*

But wait! Stop just for a moment and consider how useful the lock screen can be to you if correctly configured. Remember that it's the first thing you look at but the time in which you're doing so can set you up for the next tasks you'll perform.

In the Settings panel, which you access by clicking the gear icon above the Power button in the bottom-left corner of the Start menu, under *Personalization* ➤ *Lock screen*, you can configure apps to display useful information (see Figure 5-2).

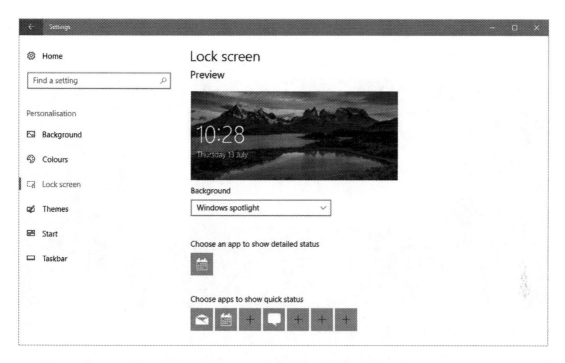

Figure 5-2. You can configure the lock screen to display useful information

This includes one app that can show detailed information, and another seven to display a counter. In the example here, the Calendar is set to display full information. This means that at a glance I can immediately see if I have anything coming that day. Below that, I only have three apps displaying information.

This might have been the way I wanted it set up, but properly configured, you can see at a glance the number of emails, instant messages, alerts, text messages, and notifications from financial or other business apps that you have waiting for you. All of this information helps you determine, at a glance, what you want to prioritize and what might end up being a time-sink if you dive into it too early.

Organizing Your Workspace

Okay, so you've dismissed the lock screen, are safely ignoring the huge mass of email that can only mean some crisis or another has arisen, that everybody will be looking to you to sort, and you're now staring at a blank desktop. Now what?

Well, you open apps, right? You open Outlook and other Office apps, such as Excel or PowerPoint. When you open your customer relationship manager, or finance or reporting app, you almost definitely open a web browser, such as Microsoft Edge or Google Chrome, or an app such as Microsoft Teams.

Within a couple of minutes, your workspace can become a complete jumbled mess of apps, meaning that you can find it confusing about what's what, what's where, and what just went bing!

In Chapter 3, I showed you how to use two really helpful features within Windows 10 to organize your desktop. The first was Snap!. This allows you to pin up to four windows (per monitor) to your desktop and dynamically resize them to make sure that all four are visible at any time.

After that came *virtual desktops*, which creates separate working environments (or hides eBay and Angry Birds from the boss, obviously). You could use these separate virtual desktops to have one desktop for communications and email, another for a specific project you're working on, and a third for general additive clutter.

Figure 5-3 shows my working desktops at the moment I'm writing this chapter. There are three virtual desktops. The first desktop contains the Word document that I'm using for this chapter and a File Explorer window in which I can easily access the other chapters I've written, images, and related files.

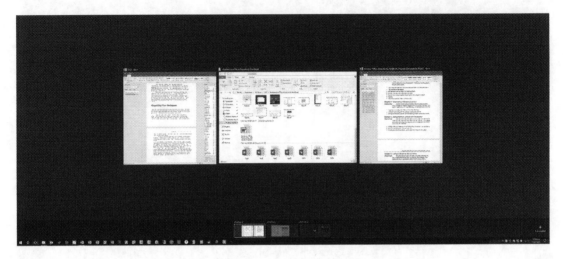

Figure 5-3. *Virtual desktops can help you organize apps*

The second desktop contains Outlook and my web browser. The third desktop (which you can't see very well here) contains the Groove Music app, which is currently playing the excellent chill out/electronica album *Suzuki* by Tosca (useful work music, and a change from my usual Jean-Michel Jarre).

This setup means that each environment is separated in a meaningful way so as to minimize distraction, and to help me concentrate on the most important tasks, such as bringing in enough money to keep my dogs in the fashion to which they have become accustomed. And believe me, they're extremely pampered pooches.

This setup also helps prevent me from casually flicking open my web browser and clicking through gaming forums or tech and political news sites. And if you think these are a time-sink, don't even think about opening a Facebook tab.

Managing Virtual Desktops

So now you're organized, but you could still be working more efficiently and effectively. For this, you can use keyboard shortcuts to very quickly and easily switch between all these running apps and desktops. Here's how...

- *Snap an app left or right.* Press the Windows key + Left and Right cursor keys to snap an app to the left or right of your screen

- *Snap an app up or down.* Press the Windows key + the Up or Down cursor keys to move a snapped app to the top or bottom left or right corner of the screen

- *Resize snapped apps.* Grab the edges of a snapped app to resize it; but for left and right snapped apps, it resizes the other app to ensure that the screen is full at all times.

- *Create a new virtual desktop.* Press the Windows key + Ctrl + D.

- *Switch between virtual desktops.* Press the Windows key + Ctrl + the Left or Right cursor keys.

- *Close the current app.* Press the Windows key + F4.

- *Minimize all the windows on your desktop at once.* Swipe downward on your laptop's trackpad with three fingers. Swipe upward with three fingers to restore the windows.

There is a full list of all keyboard shortcuts for Windows 10 in Appendix A. A list of Windows 10 touch and trackpad gestures is in Appendix B.

Where the Heck Did I Put that Report?

Okay, so your desktop is organized. Big whoop! This is great, but it's pretty useless if you can't find that damn report you were just working on, and that has to be on the client's desk this afternoon.

You can open the File tab in Word, Excel or another Office 365 app to display a list of recently accessed documents. This can be a good way to access the file, but anything that requires more than two clicks to open a file is, let's face it, inefficient and time-consuming.

I've loved the Jump List feature ever since it was first introduced in Windows 7. I use it all the time, every single day. This feature is invoked by right-clicking, or touching and holding, an icon on the taskbar to display a menu (see Figure 5-4).

Figure 5-4. *Jump Lists are a great way to get quick access to files*

The items that appear in a Jump List vary according to the app, but they can include recently opened files, create a new file, send a message or an email, create a new calendar appointment, and much more.

What I personally find most useful is the ability to pin files and documents to the Jump List. When you move your cursor over the file list, you see a pin icon appear to the right of each item. Clicking this pin icon pins or unpins a file to the Jump List. Pinning files and documents is a great way to make sure that they are *always* available to open with just two clicks, a real time-saver.

Hey, Cortana… Where the Heck Did I Put that Report?

Alas, speaking this into Cortana in Windows 10 will merely open a web search for "Where the heck did I put that report?" which isn't massively helpful, but that's because Cortana isn't intelligent enough to know what you mean by "that report"… at least not yet! Microsoft's artificial intelligence researchers are working on it, though.

What you can do is ask Cortana for specific searches; typing these into Cortana also works. A search for "Show me all documents about Claridge's" (my dog likes it there) uses intelligent search to search not only file names, but also the text within documents, emails, contacts, and more to provide results (see Figure 5-5).

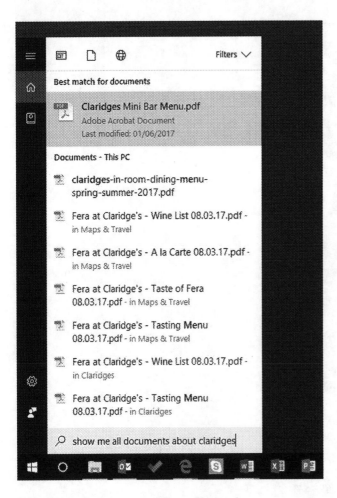

Figure 5-5. *Cortana uses intelligent file search*

As I mentioned in Chapter 2, you can use the *Filters* feature in the top-right corner of the search results window to further refine your search. This means you can filter the search to videos, web search, or just folders on the PC.

Cortana is capable of performing some highly intelligent, natural language search. In Figure 5-6, you see a search for "Show me documents I'm currently working on." Cortana interprets this query correctly, and displays a list of all the documents that have been created or opened in the last few days, with the document I have worked on most recently, this chapter, highlighted at the top of the list.

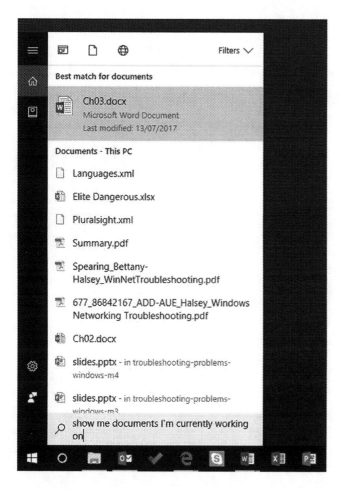

Figure 5-6. *Cortana can perform very intelligent, natural language search*

It's worth experimenting with Cortana to see what she's capable of, as new functionality is added a couple of times a year with updates to Windows 10.

Summary

Being organized is one thing, and Cortana and the basic search functionality is great, but many of us build up huge volumes of files and documents, and just working on a project at work can end up producing many more documents itself. Navigating your way through all of this can be daunting, so in the next chapter, we're going to delve into the advanced search and retrieval facilities available in Windows 10.

CHAPTER 6

Using Search to Keep Yourself Organized

If you really want to search in Windows 10, then File Explorer is the place to be. File Explorer contains a search box near its top-right corner.

When you click in the search box, a Search tab appears on the ribbon at the top of the window. This tab contains useful search parameters that you can use, such as searching by file type, size, or the last date the file was opened and modified. A *Recent Searches* drop-down menu is also available.

You can perform basic searches here, by just typing a word of name, or you can use Advanced Query Syntax (AQS) to perform more detailed and complex searches.

These AQS searches might appear sometimes to be overly complex and difficult, but it doesn't have to be as if you can remember some of the basic search commands, File Explorer helps you with the rest, as it pops out helpful options and menus to assist (see Figure 6-1).

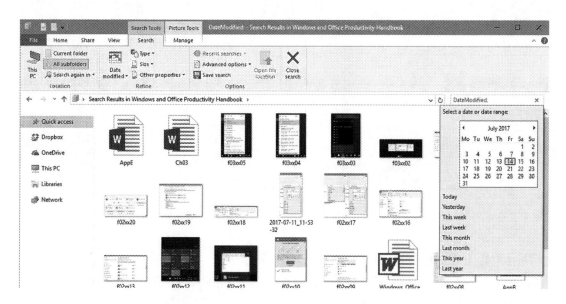

Figure 6-1. *Advanced search functionality can be found in File Explorer*

© Mike Halsey 2017
M. Halsey, *The Windows 10 Productivity Handbook*, https://doi.org/10.1007/978-1-4842-3294-1_6

I've included a complete list of File Explorer's AQS syntax in Appendix C, but as a basic primer, here are some of the more common and more useful commands.

- *Type*: allows you to search for a specific file or document type. The options are Calendar, Communication, Contact, Document, Email, [RSS] Feed, Folder, Game, Instant Message, Journal, Link, Movie, Music, Note, Picture, Playlist, Program, Recorded TV, Saved Search, Task, Video, Web History, and Unknown.

- *Date:/DateModified:/Modified*: permits different date searches. You can use Date in Date:<27/03/2017 format to search for items saved before a date, or *Date:>* to search for items saved after a date. Additionally, you can use Date: with Today, Yesterday, This week, Last week, Next month, and Last month options.

- *Size*: can be used to filter documents by their size. Options are Empty (0KB), Tiny (0 > 10KB), Small (10KB > 100KB), Medium (100KB > 1MB), Large (1MB > 16MB), Huge (16MB > 128MB), Gigantic (> 128MB).

- *Boolean operators*, such as NOT and OR, can be used to narrow your search and you can put something in quotes (" ") to search for it as a complete string.

■ **Tip**   Appendix C includes a full list of all the Advanced Query Syntax (AQS) for search in Windows 10.

Using Saved Searches in Windows 10

By far one of my all-time favorite tips in Windows is that you can save your searches and use them over, and over again. This can be especially useful. Clicking *Save search* (see Figure 6-2) saves the search as a file on your PC; you can save it anywhere. When you double-click the saved search later to open it, the search dynamically updates so that it's not just a snapshot of the search as it was at the time you saved it, but accurately reflects all the changes, deletions, and additions made to files and documents on the PC.

Figure 6-2. *You can save searches in File Explorer*

Configuring Search in Windows 10

Searching for files and documents in Windows 10 can either be lightning fast or slow as hell. This is because the operating system maintains an "index" that contains information on every file, and the keywords within or associated with them.

Sometimes you might find that a location you want to search, such as a second hard disk in the PC, isn't included in the index. As such, it takes an age to search, as the search has to be performed from scratch, with no help.

You can manage the index on your PC and control which folders, files, and disks are included. To do this, search in the Start Menu for **search** and open *Change how Windows searches* from the results. This opens the *Indexing Options* panel (see Figure 6-3).

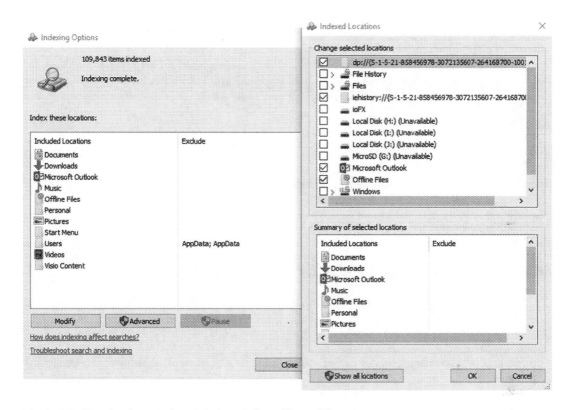

Figure 6-3. *You can change where Windows indexes files and documents*

The Indexing Options panel lists the disks and folders that are indexed on the PC, which includes your user folders (Documents, Music, Pictures, etc.) and other standard locations, such as your email.

If you click the *Modify* button, a more complete list of disks and folders on the PC appears, where you can check (or uncheck) the ones you want included in, or excluded from the index. If your disk location isn't appearing in the list, click the *Show all locations* button to display any that may be hidden.

■ **Note** You cannot add network drives and storage to the Windows Index unless you create a symbolic link between your PC and the network storage. You can do this in a Command Prompt window with the mklink command. It's a bit complex, but if you search online for **mklink**, you can find additional help. Use the format mklink /d <Link> <Target>, where the /d switch creates a directory symbolic link, by default, only a file symbolic link is created. <Link> and <Target> are the names of the Symbolic link folders that appear on your PC, and the actual directory on the remote storage; for example, as this is a bit complex, mklink /d \MyDocs \\Users\User1\Documents. You can read more about Symbolic Links at http://pcs.tv/2tQeSqN.

Organizing Your Files Using Libraries

Shh! We're going to talk about Libraries. Actually, there's no need to be quiet, you can shout about Libraries from the rooftops if you like, as they can be a brilliant way to organize and find your files and documents.

Libraries is a feature of File Explorer that's hidden when you install Windows 10, although it's very easy to switch it on. You activate the Libraries feature in File Explorer by clicking the *View* tab, and then the *Navigation pane* button, which displays a *Show libraries* option (see Figure 6-4).

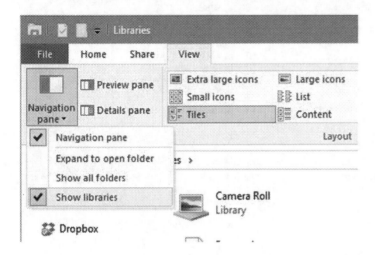

Figure 6-4. *You can activate Libraries easily*

Windows 10 creates some Libraries for you automatically, such as Documents, Pictures, and Videos. Each contains the contents of that particular user folder. However, it's the way that you can arrange and organize files and documents in Libraries that gives them such power and flexibility.

When you right-click in any blank space in a Library, the pop-up context menu that appears on screen gives you an *Arrange by* option. This is not something available in a normal File Explorer view, which only allows you to sort or group files.

The *Arrange by* options that are available to you depend on the types of files that you are looking at in the Library. For example, when looking at Documents, you can arrange your files by Author, Date Modified, Tag, Type, or Name (see Figure 6-5).

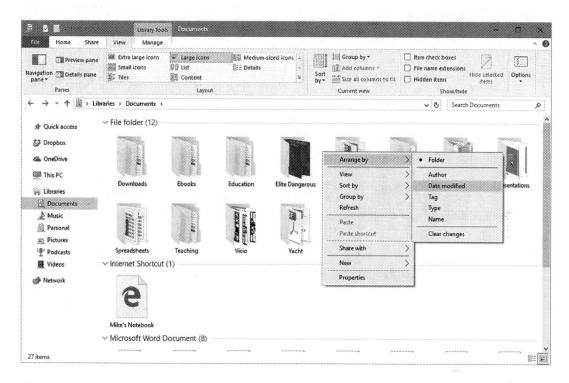

Figure 6-5. *You can arrange files in different ways in Libraries*

When you choose an *Arrange by* option, the view changes to either display the contents of the Library in an organized list format, or as a series of stacked icons (see Figure 6-6).

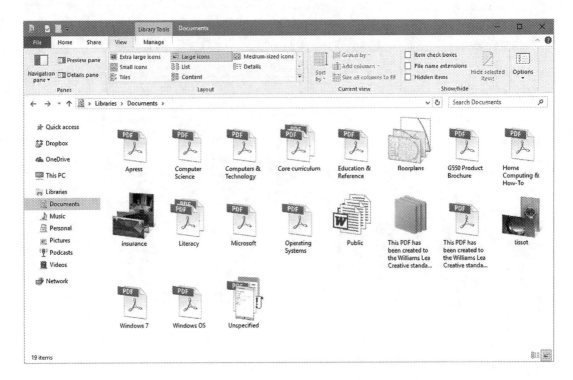

Figure 6-6. *Libraries allow you to organize your documents in different ways*

In this example, I'm arranging the files and documents by tags. Think of a tag as a search term that allows you to quickly drill down into your files and documents to find what it is you're looking for. As an example, you might use tags, such as *Contoso* to refer to files that reference a specific client account, or *Accounts* for financial documents.

You can set tags in several ways. First, you can use the Details pane in File Explorer to set them, and I'll show you how to do this shortly, or you can add tags when you save a document. When you save a document in Microsoft Office, for example, beneath the boxes where you specify the file name and file type is the *More options* link.

If you click this then a dialog appears that includes the option to set tags, a title, and a subject to the document (see Figure 6-7). The tags, title, and subject then become searchable on the PC, which makes documents easier to find.

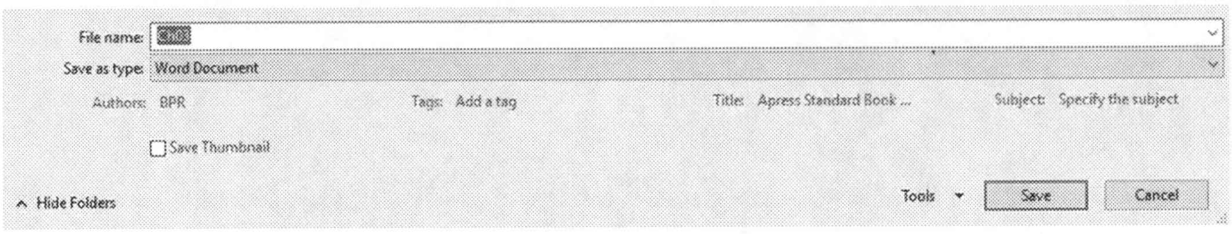

Figure 6-7. *You can add tags when you save an Office document*

Managing File and Document Tags and Details

I mentioned there was a way to edit the tags associated with a document or file by using the *Details pane*. This is available through the *View* tab on the ribbon in File Explorer, where you see a *Details pane* button near the left side. Clicking this opens the panel on the right side of the main File Explorer window, where clicking a file or document reveals details about it (see Figure 6-8).

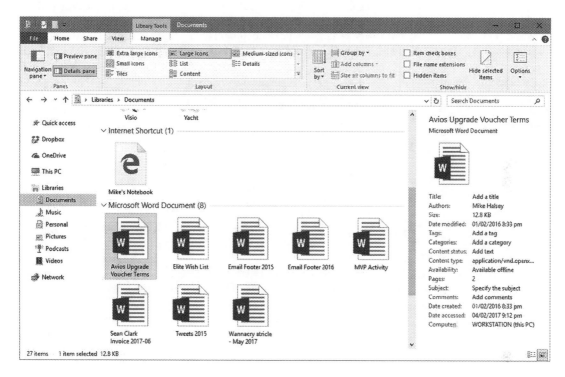

Figure 6-8. *You can view and edit details of a document or file*

Making sure that the information associated with a file or document is correct can greatly speed up the time it takes to search for, and find it. The details you are able to change for each file or document varies depending on the document or file type, but in the prior example, we can change the tags, category, content type, subject, comments, title, author, and more.

■ **Tip**　Just above the Details pane button is a *Preview pane* button. Clicking this opens a panel on the right side of File Explorer in which is displayed a preview of any supported document or file that's clicked on and highlighted. Note that not all document types are supported, you may for example use a custom file type in your place of business, but many document types, such as pictures, Microsoft Office documents, and PDF files are supported.

Sharing Files and Documents

It's one thing to be able to quickly find and effectively work with files and documents on your PC, but collaboration is really the aim of the game. Later in this book, I'll show you how to use the collaboration tools built into Microsoft Office. File Explorer contains its own collaboration tools, however, that are perhaps unsurprisingly, under the *Share* tab.

Most of the options here are self-explanatory, such as *Email*, *Zip*, *Burn to disc* (do people really still do that?), and *Fax* (see Figure 6-9). The *Share* button displays a list of Windows Store apps (which may include Microsoft Office on your PCs) that you can share the file or document with. The apps that are supported vary, but you may see common business apps, such as OneNote or Skype in the list.

Figure 6-9. *You can share documents from File Explorer*

If there is more than one user on the PC, perhaps because you hot-desk with someone else, their name appears in the *Share with* section of the tab. You can click their name, and that person is then able to access and open the file in their own account.

Additionally you can share a whole folder with users on your PC, or across your network (your PC needs to be switched on for them to have access) by right-clicking it and selecting *Share with* ➤ *Specific People* from the context menu that appears.

This displays a dialog in which you can select specific users on the PC, across your network, or whole groups of users who can have access to the folder (see Figure 6-10).

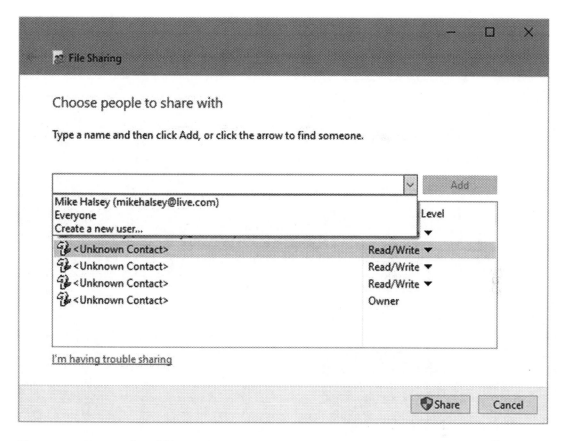

Figure 6-10. *You can share folders with users, or groups of users*

The drop-down menu displays users and user groups that have been configured on your PC and network. If you don't find a user or group here that you want to share with, you should check with your IT provisioning department to see if they've been set up to be visible to you.

When you share a folder with a user or user group this way you can change their *Permission level*, which by default is Read/Write to just Read, if you want people to be able to access a file, such as meeting notes, but not edit or delete them. It is also in this dialog that you can remove user permissions access from a folder.

Managing the Quick Access View

One thing I've not mentioned yet is the *Quick access* view in File Explorer. This is the default view and displays a list of all the files, documents, and folders that you've recently accessed.

This can be a great way to easily access your most recently used documents; however, you may not always want specific documents appearing here, especially if you people looking over your shoulder a lot. You can configure and even completely disable the Quick access panel under the View tab by clicking the *Options* button, or by opening the File tab and clicking *Change folder and search options* (both things take you to the same place). This opens a dialog containing various options for File Explorer.

At the bottom of the *General* tab, you see *Privacy* options, which include two for quick access check boxes: *Show recently used files in Quick access* and *Show frequently used folders in Quick access* (see Figure 6-11). Additionally, the *Clear* button allows you to quickly wipe the Quick access history.

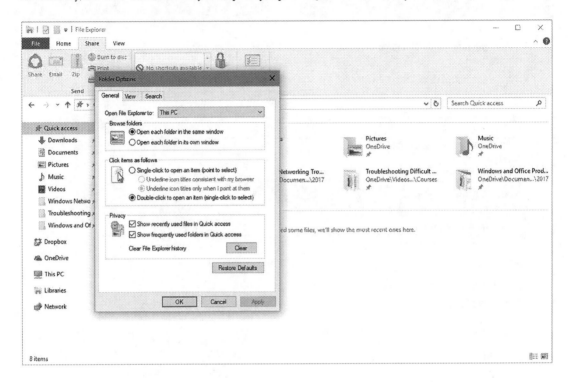

Figure 6-11. *You can configure Quick access in File Explorer*

Pinning Folders to Quick Access

You can pin folders to the Quick access panel in File Explorer to you can get easy access to them. To do this, right-click any folder, and from the context menu that appears, select *Pin to Quick access*. A quick link to that folder appears in the quick access panel to the left of File Explorer (see Figure 6-12).

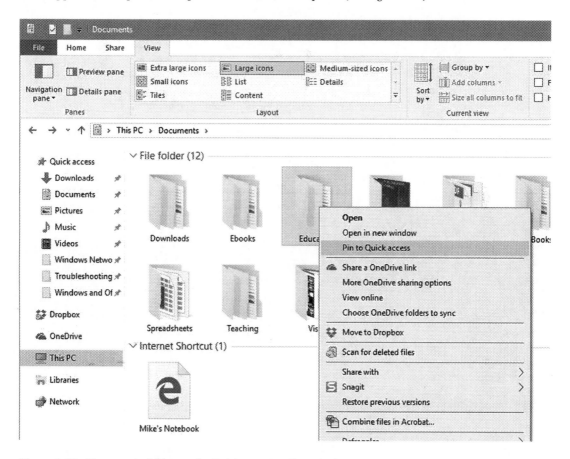

Figure 6-12. *You can pin folders to the Quick access toolbar*

Next to each pinned folder, you'll see a pin icon. You can click this icon at any time to unpin the folder, when you're finished with it and don't need quick access to it any more.

Summary

There are a great many ways you can use and configure Windows 10 to make your working life simpler and easier to manage. Libraries have always been a keen favorite of mine. I use them almost every day.

You'll have noticed that in these first few chapters, I've referred quite a bit to Settings changes you can make within Windows 10, but there are many more that you might find useful. In the next chapter, we'll look at the Settings that are available to you and how to navigate them, what you might want to change and configure, and how they can help you become more productive.

■ ■ ■

CHAPTER 7

Managing Windows Settings and Configuration

Throughout this book, I've shown you settings in Windows 10 that you can change, that can make using your PC simpler, and help make you more productive. Microsoft Windows is *the most* highly configurable and customizable operating system there's ever been. Literally everything from the way the desktop looks, to how long your battery lasts can be configured in some way.

It's not difficult to change Windows settings to be how you want them either, as Microsoft has make it simpler in Windows 10 than in any version of the operating system before it. In this chapter, we'll look at the settings you can change, examine why you'd want to, and step through how to connect your PCs to company and organization networks and file shares, no matter where you are in the world.

The Settings Panel

You'll probably be familiar with the Windows Control Panel, even if just in name. It's been the place where you've gone to change settings and configuration options ever since the first version of Windows was released in 1985.

The Control Panel is complex and difficult to use unless you're a techie and know what you're both looking for and doing. Indeed, there are many things in the Control Panel that, if you changed them, you could even render some Windows functions or apps, unusable.

With Windows 8, Microsoft set about rectifying the situation and now Windows 10 contains a much friendlier and safer place in which you can personalize the operating system—the Settings app (see Figure 7-1).

© Mike Halsey 2017

M. Halsey, *The Windows 10 Productivity Handbook*, https://doi.org/10.1007/978-1-4842-3294-1_7

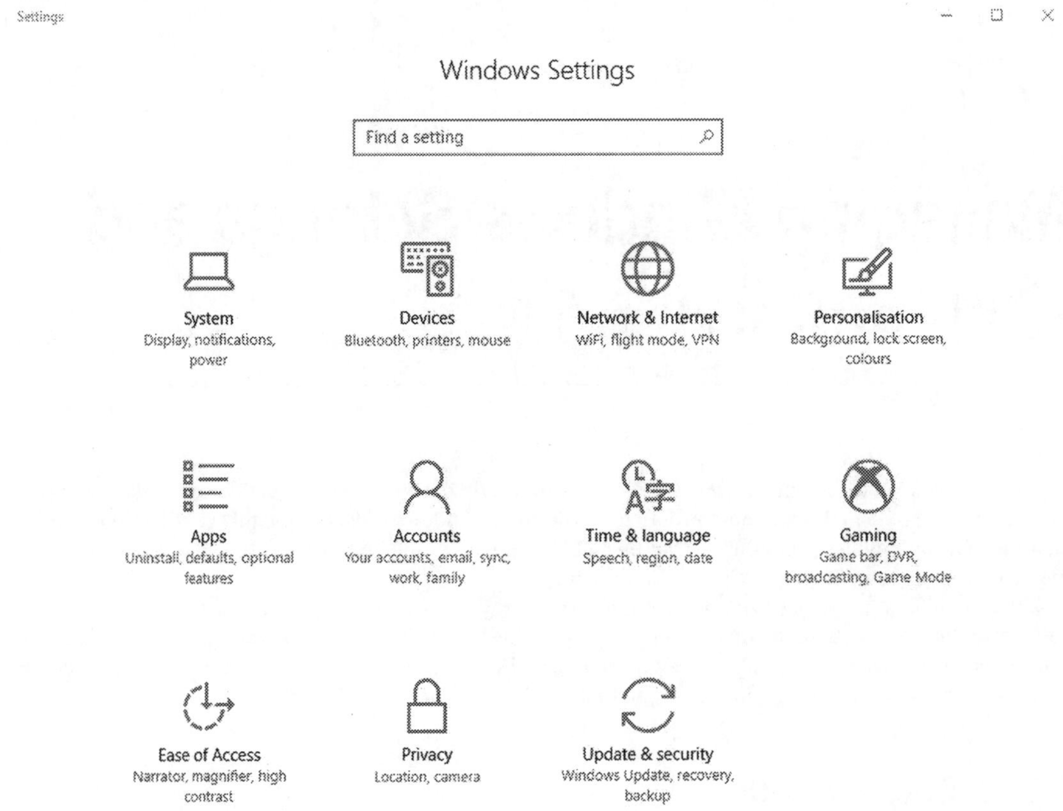

Figure 7-1. *The Settings panel in Windows 10*

You access Settings in Windows 10 by clicking the settings (cog) icon just above the Power button in the Start menu, and you'll see that settings is sensibly laid out into various categories.

- *System* is where all the settings that control your PC are located, such as the resolution of your screen, the power settings, and touch controls.

- *Devices* is where you'll find settings for any plug-in or wireless devices that your PC connects to, such as printers, your keyboard and mouse, and Bluetooth devices.

- *Network & Internet* is where you'll go to set up and manage all types of connection, from Wi-Fi to secure company connections.

- *Personalization* is something we've already looked at quite a bit. This is where you can change the look and feel of Windows 10 itself.

- *Apps* is the place where you'll control the software installed on your PC, from choosing which files open on what app, to uninstalling unwanted apps.

- *Accounts* is the location where all the user accounts that are set up on the PC are managed. It is also where you'll find parental controls and company sign-in settings.

- *Time & language* is where you'll need to go if you're travelling around the world with your laptop or tablet. It's also where you can change culturally significant settings such as currencies and numerical delimiters.

- *Gaming* is not strictly used in the workplace (wink!), but it's where you can go to set game recording, and streaming settings.

- *Ease of Access* contains all the settings that can make Windows 10 easier to use for people with cognitive, physical, visual, or auditory impairments.

▓ **Tip** Many more people than those with disabilities and difficulty using computers can benefit from the Ease of Access features. My book, *The Windows 10 Accessibility Handbook* (Apress, 2015) describes how they can be used to help everybody from young children, and the elderly, to people working in noisy environments, people who are color-blind, and people who have repetitive strain and other common injuries.

- *Privacy* allows you to control how the information about you and your PC account is shared with apps and with Microsoft.

- *Update & security* contains the settings for Windows Update, backup, recovery, and the Windows Defender antivirus service.

I won't show you around all the settings in Windows 10 because you'll never need many of them. Although I've not yet discussed them in this book, there are some settings that you can use to make your PC an easier and more pleasant place to work.

▓ **Tip** If you find the auto-correct spell checker in Windows to be inaccurate or annoying; for example, if you work in an environment such as legal, engineering, or science that uses a very specialized language, you can disable the Windows 10 spell checker in Devices ➤ Typing.

System Settings

The System settings are the first listed in the Settings panel, and so this seems like the logical place to begin. System is where you'll find all the settings associated with your PC's hardware, such as your power and battery, keyboard, mouse, and screen.

Making Your Display Easier to Use

It's very common these days for people to have laptops, tablets, and desktops with ultra-high resolution 4K or 5K screens, and for us to use those screens late at night.

Sometimes you need to change how your display works so that you avoid eyestrain, getting tired, or getting headaches, and also to help you get to sleep afterward. Fortunately, Windows 10 includes features for all of this.

The *System* ➤ *Display* options begin with a handy feature called *Night light* (see Figure 7-2).

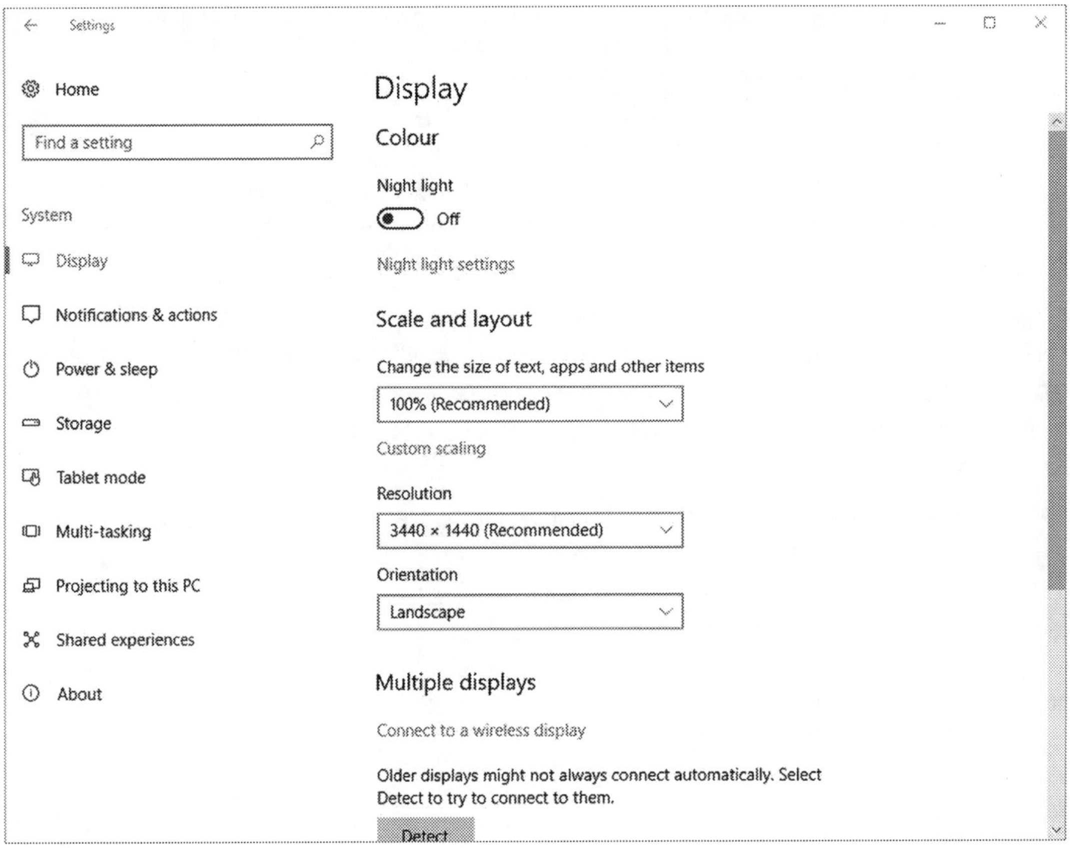

Figure 7-2. *There are multiple Display settings available*

Night light adjusts the blue light from your screen as the evening and night progress. This gives the screen a yellower and softer look, which puts less strain on your eyes and allows you to relax more, ultimately helping you sleep.

Below the Night light option, you can change the text scaling on your screen. This can be helpful if you sometimes, or often, find text and other things difficult to read. The scaling options vary from 100% all the way on PCs with high-resolution displays up to 225%.

Just one more thing of note, is that if you use projectors regularly with your PC, for meetings or other events, or if you use more than one monitor with your PC, the multiple monitor and wireless projector display options are also to be found here.

Managing Notifications

In Chapter 2, I showed you how to use the Notifications settings to keep your PC quiet during times when you'd rather not be disturbed. There's more you can do to configure notifications accessed through the System settings.

Everything wants to tell you something these days. From your email, to instant messaging, your calendar, Cortana, your web browser, social media, and smartphone, through to individual apps, app updaters, file sharing, cloud backup and on it goes. The cacophony can be quite overwhelming sometimes, and truly annoying at others.

The *Notifications & actions* panel in the System settings allows you control and tame all notifications, and notifications from individual apps and programs on the PC (see Figure 7-3).

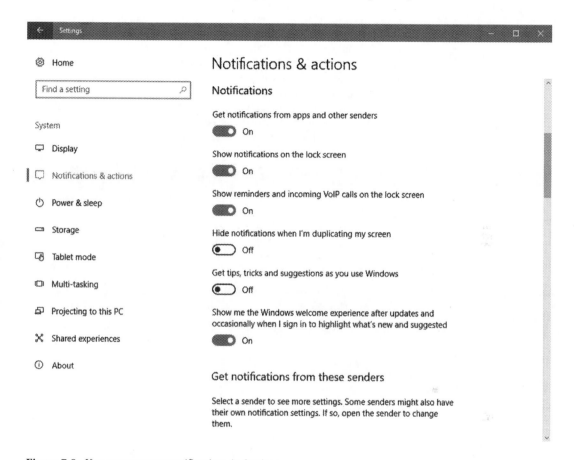

Figure 7-3. *You can manage notifications in Settings*

The first option, *Get notifications from apps and other senders*, allows you to turn all app and program notifications on or off globally.

If you never want to be bothered by Notifications, this is the switch to change. Scroll down the list and you'll see on/off switches for every app and program installed on the PC that can create alerts. If Adobe Creative Cloud or Spotify is annoying you, completely turn off their notifications. Have you been wondering why the financial alerts you set up haven't been appearing, turn them back on, and so on, and so forth.

▓ **Tip**   Conversely, you might think that the default notification display period of 5 seconds isn't long enough for you to read what they say. You can change this setting in *Ease of Access, Other Options* where a drop-down menu has display periods ranging from 5 seconds to 5 minutes.

Power to the People!

If you get annoyed that your PC goes to sleep, or the display keeps turning off when you've only been away from the machine for a couple of minutes, the *Power & sleep* settings in the System settings section is here to save the day. I'll discuss these in greater depth in Chapter 9, but it's worth going over the basics here.

Why is this important? Well, realistically speaking, it's little gripes and annoyances—such as the PC going to sleep, restarting, or turning off when you don't want it to—that can build up frustration in a person, eventually meaning that some get to a position where they'll end up resenting their working environment and the PC. This isn't good for either productivity or your state of mind.

At its simplest, the power settings just let you choose when the screen switches off, and when the PC goes to sleep. These settings are different for mobile devices (laptops, and tablets) and desktop PCs, which don't have a battery, and they're quite simple and straightforward to use and set (see Figure 7-4).

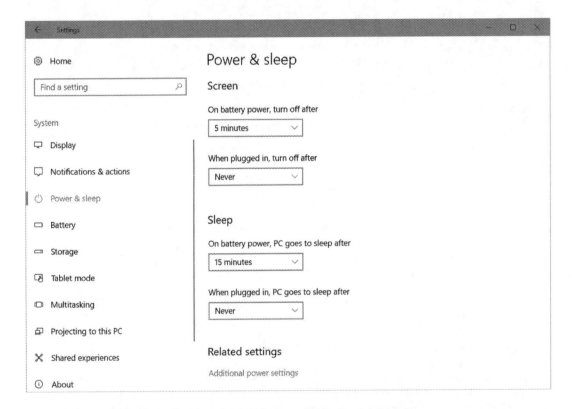

Figure 7-4. *You can change when the computer sleeps or the display switches off*

For mobile devices, you also see a *Battery* settings section (see Figure 7-5). Some of the settings here can be especially useful. There is a slider to control the *Battery saver* mode. This allows the PC to effectively go into low power, but still working state when the battery level drops below a certain level, 20% by default. What this means is that the screen dims (this is an optional setting) and all background tasks, such as the updating of live tiles, and apps updating themselves from the Internet will stop.

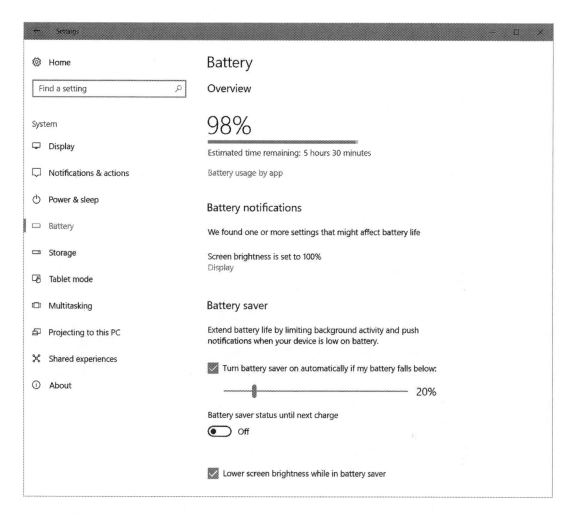

Figure 7-5. *The Battery settings allow additional power control*

▓ **Tip**   If you notice your battery is draining faster that you expect it should, click the *Battery usage by app* link. This displays a list of all the installed desktop and store apps on your PC in a bar chart that shows which ones are the most power-hungry. You can use this to determine what you want to uninstall, replace with an alternative app, or close when it's not needed.

Back in the *Power & sleep* settings, you'll see an *Additional power settings* link. Now if you click this, you'll be presented with the older-style Power options in the Control Panel. But hang on a second because there's some cool stuff in here that might benefit you.

Clicking the *Choose what the power buttons do* link in the top-left corner of the window allows you choose what Power and Sleep do (assuming that your laptop features them) (see Figure 7-6).

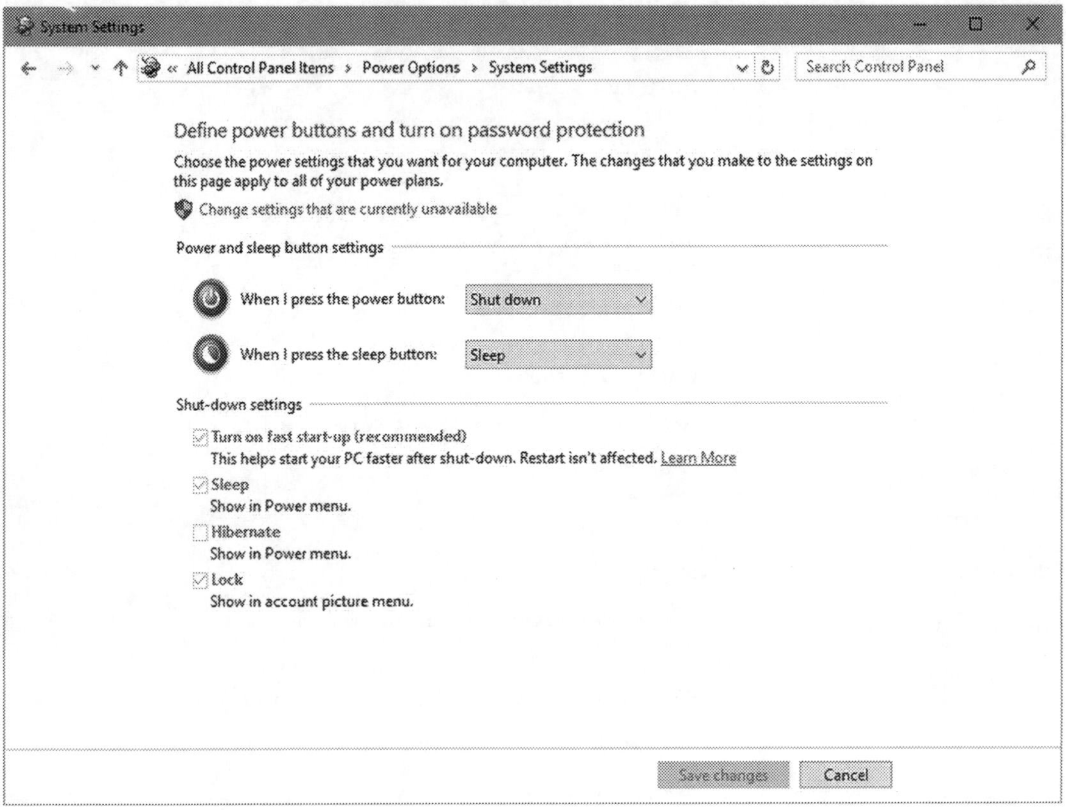

Figure 7-6. *You can choose an action for the Power button*

The first thing you'll notice is that you'll need to click the *Change settings that are currently unavailable* link, as all the most useful options are grayed out.

The main attraction is the ability to reprogram the power and sleep buttons on the PC. Why might you want to do this? Well back in the days of PCs of old, they were very bad at sleeping (I know the feeling, Ed.) but advances in modern hardware have improved things considerably. This means that even the biggest desktop PC might benefit from sleep or hibernation, rather than being shut down. But what is the difference between Sleep and Hibernate anyway?

- *Sleep* puts the PC into a low-power state, but keeps your programs and apps alive in the computer's memory. Sleep does use power; once you disconnect it, the contents of the memory will be lost (a volatile storage medium).

- *Hibernate* saves the memory file on the PC to your hard disk (which is a non-volatile storage medium) and then turns off the power to the PC. This is slower to resume than sleep, as memory is significantly faster than even the fastest hard disk, but doesn't consume any power when in its off state.

- *Fast Start-up* is a sort of hybrid system. It's not supported on all PC hardware, so it may not be available on your PC. It works by signing off all the users on the PC, and then saving the rest of the memory state to the hard disk. Think of it as halfway between Hibernation and Off completely.

By default, Fast Start-up is how Windows 10 always turns off, if your hardware allows it. However, you might not always want this feature enabled. For example, if you find that some Windows Updates aren't being installed, this is because Fast Start-up doesn't perform a "proper" shutdown, which Windows Update requires on some PCs.

Additionally, some third-party file and disk encryption technologies complain mightily, or just fail to work correctly with Fast Start-up. If you have a dual-boot system installed on your PC, such as two versions of Windows that you can boot between, or Windows and Linux, then Fast Start-up might also interfere with that.

Back in the main Control Panel, there are the *Power Options*. Clicking either *Choose when to turn off the display* or *Change when the computer sleeps* displays the *Change [the] advanced power settings* link.

This displays a dialog with many more options, some of which you might find useful (see Figure 7-7). For example, you might find that telling your hard disk to turn off earlier than the default 20 minutes saves some battery power.

Figure 7-7. *There are many advanced power settings*

Additionally, you could find that after the PC has been left unattended for a while, one of your USB devices fails to operate. Changing the power settings for the USB sleep system can rectify this.

There are other options here that you might to explore; a potentially useful one is to throttle back the *Maximum processor state*, which is set at 100% by default. If you have a particularly powerful processor in your computer, or a particularly undemanding workload, you can throttle the processor back to a smaller percentage of its overall potential; let's say down to 80%. This can sometimes have a significant effect on improving the battery life of your PC.

Keep Taking the Tablets!

Are you using a hybrid tablet device for work, such as a Microsoft Surface Pro or a Lenovo Yoga? If so, then you'll likely be familiar with what happens when you detach your keyboard, or flip the screen all the way around to hide the keyboard. Windows 10 automatically flips to Tablet mode.

This is a special mode of the operating system where the focus is put on pen and touch input, instead of mouse and keyboard. You'll notice icons get further apart (the ribbon icons in Office become more spaced out as well, which you might find generally more useful), and the Start menu expands to fill your whole screen.

What can be more annoying is all the icons that you have pinned to the taskbar can disappear! The Tablet mode settings allow you to customize this and other actions, so switching to Tablet mode doesn't mean your taskbar icons have to disappear (see Figure 7-8). Additionally, you can disable Tablet mode completely if you don't want it, or enable it all the time if you find features such as the extra spacing between icons useful.

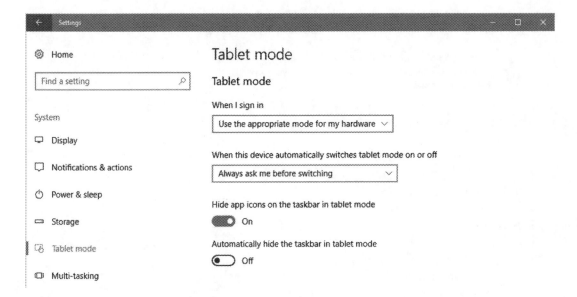

Figure 7-8. *You can configure Tablet mode in Settings*

How to Win at Snap!

Back in Chapter 3, I talked about how you can use the snap and virtual desktop features of Windows 10 to improve your workflow. You'll find the configuration options for these two features in *Multitasking* in the System settings (see Figure 7-9).

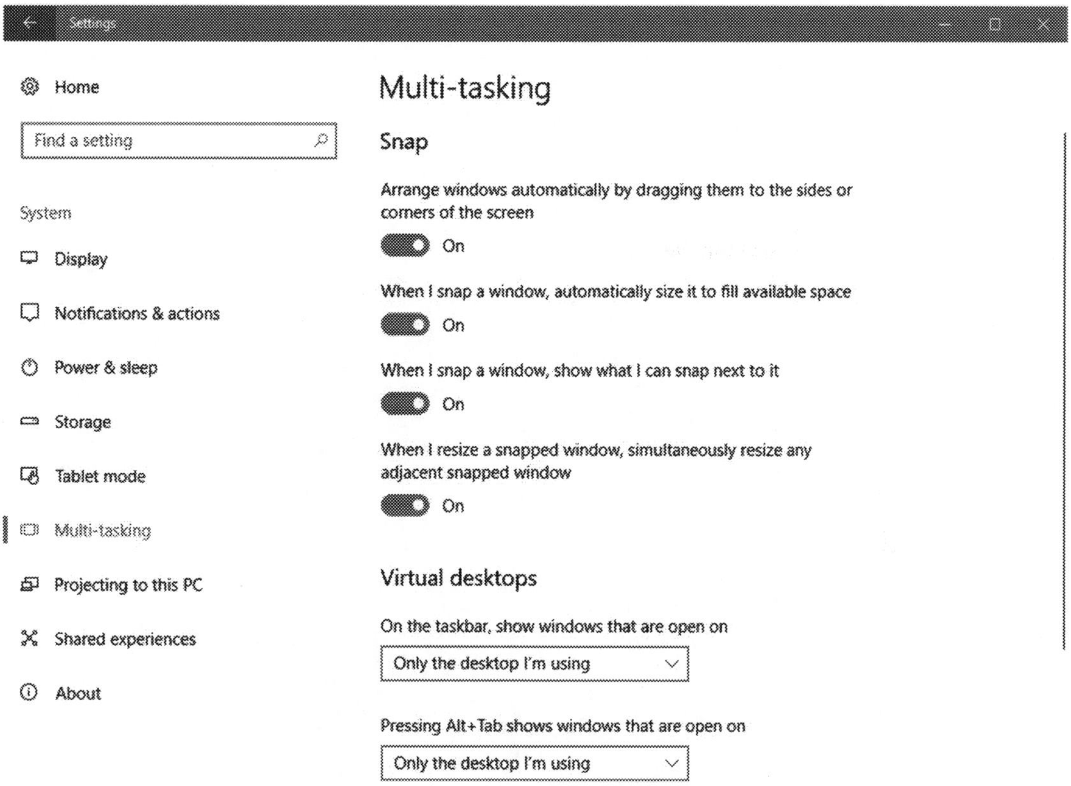

Figure 7-9. *You can configure Windows snap and virtual desktops*

Why might you want to do this? If you're a little shaky with the mouse, or if you use multiple monitors with your PC, or if snap doesn't work properly for you, you may want to disable it.

The arrangement of taskbar icons can also be annoying when using multiple desktops, as the default setting is to only show taskbar icons for apps that are running on the desktop you are using, instead of all virtual desktops. Changing this setting can make it much easier to switch between different apps and desktops.

Summary

The number of settings and options available in Windows 10 are vast, which can be daunting, so I've highlighted all the ones that are of most use. This doesn't mean that when you have some free time, you can't look around to see what else is available to make using Windows 10 more pleasurable and make you more productive.

Some settings can appear pretty complex but still utterly essential, such as those to manage your hardware devices, and networks. In the next chapter, I'll show you how to tame and take control of these and more.

CHAPTER 8

Managing Network Connections and Devices

Nobody can use a PC effectively without the ability to print, use USB and other hardware devices, or access networks and the Internet. Here we begin to deal with the more complex subjects that can appear daunting.

This doesn't need to be the case, because it's far simpler than you might think to take control of the devices and networks you need to use.

Managing Hardware Devices

The *Devices* settings in the main panel of the Settings app are—you'll be unsurprised to hear—where you can manage all the external hardware devices that you attach to your PC, such as printers and Bluetooth headsets.

Managing Your Default Printers

If you use your laptop or tablet in more than one place, which is fairly likely, then you'll probably have come up against the problem of documents failing to print because you've sent the job to a printer that's actually located in another building, somewhere else in the country.

© Mike Halsey 2017

M. Halsey, *The Windows 10 Productivity Handbook*, https://doi.org/10.1007/978-1-4842-3294-1_8

Windows 10 is clever in the way it manages multiple printers, and in the *Devices* ➤ *Printers & scanners*, settings you'll find a check box option to *Let Windows manage my default printer* (see Figure 8-1).

Figure 8-1. *Windows can manage your default printers for you*

This works quite simply by setting the default printer for each of the different wired of Wi-Fi networks you connect to, based on what you have tended to use on that network in the past. This means that for the first one or two times that you use a printer at a new location, you'll need to choose the printer manually. After that, Windows intelligently associates printers with the local network, and then changes the default printer accordingly when you move from place to place.

▓ **Tip**   If you find the autocorrect spell checker in Windows to be inaccurate or annoying (for example, you work in an environment such as legal, engineering, or science, which uses very specialized language), you can disable the Windows 10 spell checker in Devices ➤ Typing.

Managing USB Device AutoPlay

I'm sure I'm not the only person in the world who finds it annoying when you plug a USB device into the PC, and Windows pops up an alert asking what you'd like to do with it. This reminds me of all those horrible times when Clippy would pop up his head in Microsoft Word to ask if you're writing a letter, though I'm sure you'll be delighted to hear that Clippy and I have since made up and become great friends (see Figure 8-2).

Figure 8-2. *Clippy and I have worked together now on several occasions*

The settings to allow you to choose what happens when you plug USB devices into your PC can be found in *Devices* ➤ *AutoPlay*. They're separated into different sections, for Removable drives, Memory cards, and other devices such as your phone, and you might find you want to either open a specific app, or to disable actions completely (see Figure 8-3).

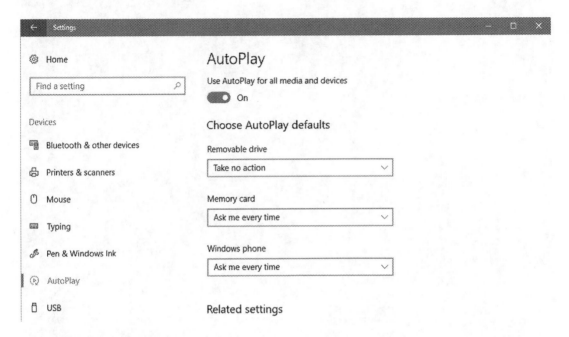

Figure 8-3. *You can choose what happens when you plug USB devices into your PC*

Network and Internet

The *Network & Internet* settings are where you can do really boring, or unwanted things, such as connect to the company or organization network, or configure the company's security settings for their Virtual Private Network. Yeah, tell me about it, nothing fun here.

Managing Wi-Fi Networks

Connecting to Wi-Fi networks is simple… right? Well, not always as sometimes something might go wrong, such as the settings for a Wi-Fi network becoming corrupt, or perhaps because you've accidentally hit the button that allows all the other devices connected to the network to see your PC, when you should have said, keep my PC private and hidden.

The *Network & Internet* ➤ *WiFi* settings enable you to effectively manage your Wi-Fi networks. Clicking the *Manage known networks* link enables you to tell Windows 10 to *Forget* a network for which the settings are incorrect or corrupt (see Figure 8-4).

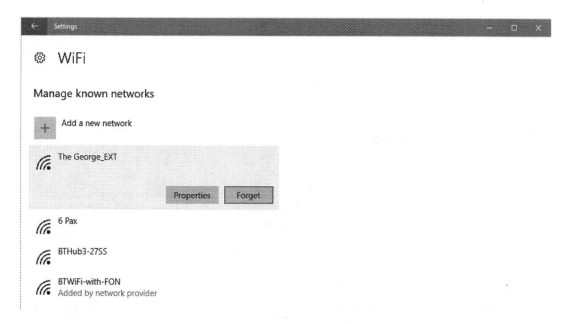

Figure 8-4. *You can tell Windows 10 to Forget Wi-Fi networks*

The Wi-Fi settings also allow you to choose what happens when you're near public Wi-Fi services, such as in bars and coffee shops. It may be that, for security reasons, you really don't want your PC connecting to these networks. Fortunately, Windows 10 makes it very easy to turn this functionality off completely.

Managing VPN Connections

Virtual Private Networks (VPNs) are special secure connections that create a "private" company or organization network over a "public" or otherwise insecure network, such as home broadband. It achieves this by encrypting all the data sent and received, and diverting all traffic through a specialized, encrypted, Internet server somewhere in the world.

It is this encryption and routing that hides all information about the connection from the Internet Service Provider (ISP) you are connecting through, and that has made VPNs popular with world travelers who want to maintain access to the video-on-demand services they pay for at home (though you should always be aware that some VPN use can violate the terms of service for some streaming providers). It is why VPNs have come to the attention of countries like the United Arab Emirates, China, and Russia, who have banned them.

If you need to set up a VPN connection on your PC, laptop, or tablet, then you were already provided with all the connection information you need from your business or organization. However, I want to make a special note here about security and law enforcement.

■ **Caution**   If you are travelling abroad with your laptop or tablet and need to use a VPN, check before you travel if this is legal at your destination. Some countries, such as China, the United Arab Emirates, and Russia have banned their use, and using a VPN could land you with a heavy fine, or even a short period of imprisonment.

Additional Network Settings

The rest of the network settings don't each require their own section here, as they're all small, but still significant. Below the VPN settings, you'll find an option for *Flight mode*. Yup, you guessed it: this is the essential setting you must enable before you fly.

It's actually really important to remember to flick Airplane mode on your laptop or tablet, especially if you put your PC to sleep rather than shut it down. This is because in Sleep in Windows 10 occasionally wakes the PC in order to perform actions such as checking your email and updating live tiles in the Start menu. This, naturally, activates the Wi-Fi connection and... well, hopefully there's not a big crash.

Mobile hotspot is best used on PCs that include a cellular connection that can be shared with up to ten other PCs and mobile device. They don't have to be running Windows 10 either, as anything that connects to Wi-Fi is able to connect to the hotspot that you create.

On the subject of sharing your cellular connection, the *Data usage* option can be incredibly useful to see just how much data you're using on your PC, and what apps might be hogging bandwidth. You can see this in the *Data usage* settings, where you'll be given an overview of how much data you've used on each different network type in the last 30 days (Wi-Fi, Ethernet, cellular). Below this is a *View usage details* link. Clicking this displays detailed information on each app on your PC that has been using data and how much (see Figure 8-5).

Figure 8-5. *You can see which apps are hogging bandwidth*

Apps and Features

Ending the last section by talking about apps leads very nicely into the next Settings section, where there are options that you might find useful.

Making Your PC More Secure

Security is the most important thing with your PCs, files, and data these days, right!? If you're using a PC that runs Windows 10 S, then you'll only be able to download and install apps from the Windows Store.

This might seem like a massive limitation, but it's not anywhere near as bad as you think. Microsoft has released tools that allow many older desktop (called Win32) apps to be included in the store. Initially this began with iTunes, Spotify, and the Office 365 suite of programs, and it's expanding all the time.

The advantage of only allowing and installing apps from the Store is that the PC is fundamentally more secure as a result. All Store apps are "sandboxed" in that they're completely separated and isolated from the operating system, other apps, and your files. They can't do any harm to the PC as a result, especially given that all apps submitted to the Store are tested for malware infections.

Malware almost always comes in the form of Win32 code, so if you don't allow that type of code to run and install, it's significantly harder to get any malicious code on the PC.

You can set this manually in Windows 10 Pro in the *Apps ➤ Apps & features* settings, from the *Installing apps* drop-down menu. By default, you can *Allow apps from anywhere,* but if you can live with just the store, choosing *Allow apps from the Store only* definitely beefs up the security on your PC (see Figure 8-6).

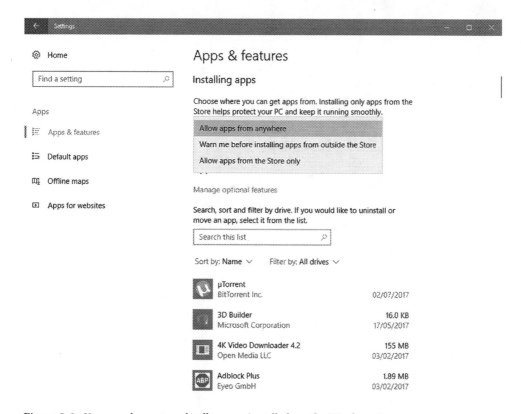

Figure 8-6. You can choose to only allow app installs from the Windows Store

Default Apps

Hands up everybody who's ever tried to open a file or document and it's either not opened at all or it has opened in the wrong program. Yup, there's a lot us. And I count myself in this because it happens to everybody at some point.

If you look in *Apps* ➤ *Default apps*, you'll see a list of different common file types (Email, Maps, Music, Photos, Videos, Web, etc.) and below each one is either an icon representing the app they're set to open with, or a *Choose a default* button. You can click the icon or button to select what app you want to use for what thing.

This is a good start, but it doesn't help with Office files, PDFs, and especially not with the custom file format you use with the specialist software you need at work. Below this list sits three links, two of which are useful.

Choose default applications by file type will display a list of all the different types of file known to your PC. These are all in the format .xyz, the three or four letters after the end of the file that signify it's type, such as .doc, .docx (Word), .xls, .xlsx (Excel), .pdf (Adobe Portable Document Format) and so on (see Figure 8-7).

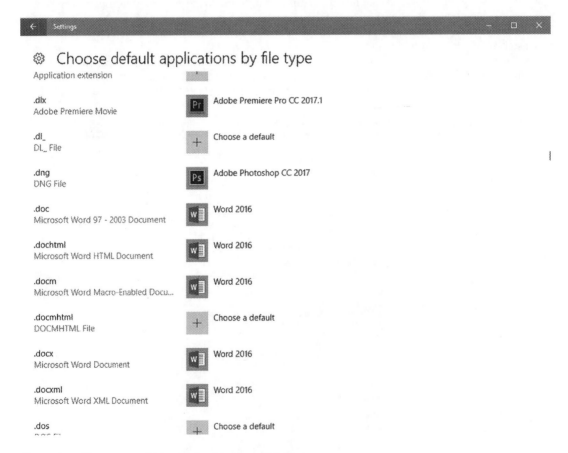

Figure 8-7. *You can set which app should open which file type*

To set a default app for a file type, look down the list until you find the file type you need to change, and then click the icon next to it to choose the correct program.

Sometimes you won't know which file type it is that you need to change, since Windows hides the .xyz file suffix from you anyway. In this case, click the *Set defaults by app* link, which opens a panel that shows a list of all of your installed programs. You can click one to see how many of its file defaults have been set.

In the example in Figure 8-8, OneNote's desktop app has just one out of its three defaults set. Below this are options to *Set this program as default* by setting all of its defaults, or to *Choose [the] defaults for this program*, which gives you more granular control.

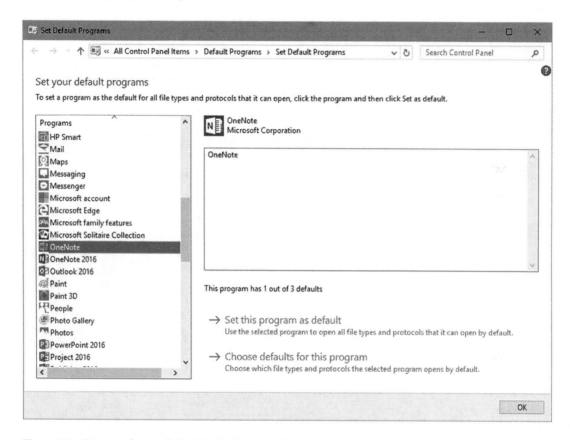

Figure 8-8. *You can choose all the defaults for a specific program*

Accounts

A little while ago, I described how you can connect to some company network types, such as VPNs, but what was missing were other account types, such as Azure AD (Active Directory). You can find this and more settings in the *Accounts* panel. There are several sections to this that you might find useful.

- *Email & app accounts* is where you can add different accounts that are used on your PC, such as work and home accounts, or different email accounts that are used by different apps.

- *Sign-in options* contains all the settings you need to change your password, set a pin or a picture password, or set up the Windows Hello biometric sign-in feature.

- *Access work or school* is where you'll find the Azure AD sign in option. You need to set this up with the settings provided by your system administrator.

▓ **Tip**   In the Sign-in options, you'll find a setting called *Dynamic lock*. If you carry a Bluetooth device with you, such as a phone, smartwatch, or even a fitness band, and pair this device with your Windows 10 PC, you can use its proximity to automatically lock and unlock your PC. This won't work with all Bluetooth devices, but it's worth trying with devices you own and use regularly.

Summary

So far throughout this book, I've explained useful settings and options that you might want to configure that can help make Windows 10 easier to use, or to help you work more effectively. This includes the Regional Settings I covered in Chapter 1, and the various Ease of Access features that I've covered throughout the first few chapters.

There are a great many additional Settings available in Windows 10, although I've focused on the ones that can help you be more productive on your PC, and offer a more pleasurable and less frustrating experience.

Now that we've tamed network connections, in the next chapter we'll take a more holistic view of your life online by looking at how you can keep yourself, your data, and the people around you safe from malware and hackers.

CHAPTER 9

■ ■ ■

Keeping Yourself and Your Data Safe and Secure

How many times have you heard a story on the news about a data breach, and that a company has lost the personal data of thousands or even millions of customers? You can probably name at least one, or remember hearing of one, straightaway.

These could have occurred through a malware infection or through a hack, because somebody in the company was tricked by a scammer or criminal into giving up a crucial password, or through another means such the theft of the data internally by an employee.

Either way the amount of data breaches you read about in the news is miniscule when compared to the number of data breaches you never get to hear about. Companies cover up these breaches, hacks, and thefts as much as they can because of the reputational damage it can do and to avoid fines that can be levied, or perhaps because they don't think the amount of data lost or stolen is "important enough" to make a fuss about.

It's important to consider when discussing computer security, that anything you do at work to keep your company and customer data safe and secure, is the same as you would do at home to keep your own personal data safe, and the same as you'd expect everybody else in any company that stores your own personal data to also do. Computer security is as much a holistic process as it is a necessary one.

Surely, I Just Install Antivirus… Right?!

Windows 10 is the most secure operating system Microsoft has ever released. The list of security features in Windows 10 is long and includes antivirus protection. So you would think that when you use your computer you'd always be safe… Sorry, but no.

Antivirus software is just a small part of a larger picture that includes work on your own part too. It's a truism in IT Support circles that nothing ever goes wrong with a computer that's left in the box and never used.

This is because nothing can ever go wrong with a computer unless a human being uses it. Thus, every problem is the ultimate result of human beings. Although some problems are traceable to a person somewhere, problems occur on their own anyway, including power spikes, component failures, or your laptop being damaged from great height by a bird.

When it comes to malware infection and hacking, however, there is plenty that you can do—and plenty that you shouldn't do. It's what you do that causes problems. To examine what I mean, it's necessary to look at how malware infections and hacking attacks work.

© Mike Halsey 2017

M. Halsey, *The Windows 10 Productivity Handbook*, https://doi.org/10.1007/978-1-4842-3294-1_9

How Do Malware Infections Happen?

Malware doesn't just appear on PCs and infect them. It simply can't do it. This is because there are multiple security systems on a PC that prevent this from happening. When you install a piece of software on your PC, or make some configuration changes, you're presented with what's called *User Account Control* (UAC) (see Figure 9-1).

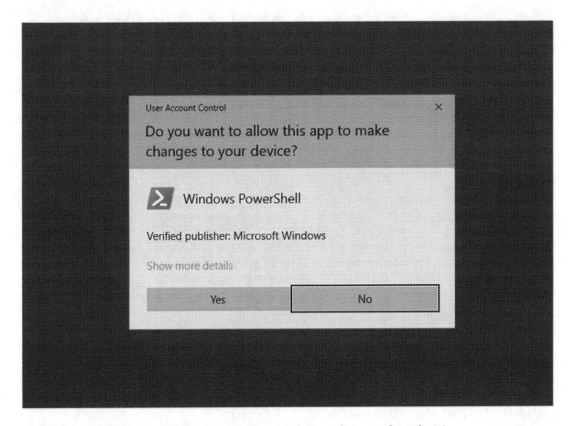

Figure 9-1. *UAC Prompts alert you when an important change is being made on the PC*

UAC is a dialog box that appears in the center of a dinned screen, telling you that you're about to do something important, and asking either for confirmation that you really want to do it, or an administrator password to confirm that you have the authority to make the change.

Windows SmartScreen might pop up an alert when you download a file from the Internet, saying that it believes opening the file, or running an installer is potentially unsafe, and asking if you *really, really* want to open it (see Figure 9-2).

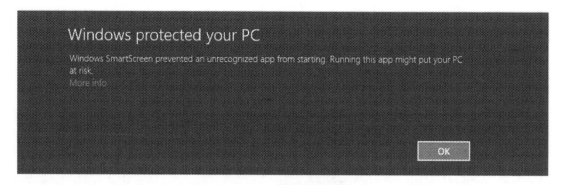

Figure 9-2. Windows SmartScreen protects against unsafe downloads

You have built-in Windows Defender Antivirus software. If it discovers malware on your PC, it alerts you with a pop-up alert in the system tray (the far right of the taskbar next to the clock) and in the Security Center (see Figure 9-3).

Figure 9-3. Windows Defender alerts you if it finds malware

So with all of this in place, and additional security features, such as the Edge web browser alerting you to and blocking known unsafe websites, you're surely perfectly safe? Well, no, unfortunately not.

There are two problems. The first of which is that antivirus software, and other security features can only scan for and identify malware that's already known to them. All antivirus packages contain *heuristic* scanning engines, that scan for "virus type" activity, but even that's no guarantee of safety and protection.

The reason for this is that zero-day malware–that is, malware that's only just been released into the wild, and hasn't been analyzed or intercepted by security researchers—can frequently cause massive infections worldwide, such as the WannaCry Ransomware in 2017, which infected computers in over 150 countries, and brought some companies and organizations, like the British National Health Service, to a standstill.

Then there's the psychology used in malware infections. You know that your PC has lots of security features designed to keep you safe, but so do the malware writers. As such, they'll try to trick you into installing the malware, by disguising it as something you want, like a game, a codec required to play a funny cat video or a file or download from a colleague. Even the hugely popular CCleaner app for Windows was compromised in 2017 by hackers when they successfully embedded malware into the installer, which was then downloaded by tens of thousands of people for several weeks before it was spotted.

It's actually common for malware to lay relatively dormant on a PC, quietly trying to infect other computers via email payloads, network attacks, and by being copied to removable devices like USB flash drives, for several weeks before making itself known to the world.

How Does Hacking Happen?

You might be aware of the term *hacking*. It's not what happens when you have a particularly bad case of catarrh. It's someone just outside your building or elsewhere in the world gaining access to your PC or company network. There are several ways that it can happen.

In the 2016 action movie *Jason Bourne*, a CIA operative gets access to a laptop that our protagonist is using. The CIA operative deletes secret files from the laptop by hacking into and getting control of a mobile phone that's in the same room. Like all the *Bourne* movies, it's brilliant to watch; but in this case, the implementation of hacking and computer security is completely nonsensical because for this scenario to work, the phone would have no on-board security and be connected to the laptop by Bluetooth or Wi-Fi that also had no security.

Given that the laptop is owned by an Edward Snowden–type character who is on the run from authorities for leaking top-secret files online, he'd have been caught long ago for being so incompetent. Having a secure laptop that's connected to Wi-Fi and the Internet at all is an automatic hacker fail!

Hacking actually works differently. It is usually done in one of two ways. The first is what's called a *brute-force attack*, in which the hacker uses software on one or many PCs to either try a massive amount of password and username combinations until they get the right one. The other, called a Denial of Service attack, floods the endpoint computer with so much traffic that it, or its software, physically fails or crashes.

If a brute force attack is allowed, then the security on the server isn't configured correctly (it should only allow a few attempts before locking). With a denial of Service attack, crashing the endpoint computer will likely block access to the hacker anyway.

What's more common is that the hacker(s) will try to gain an advantage from inside the organization. This could be system administrators using extremely weak passwords, or someone on the inside giving the hackers access.

Very occasionally, the hacker is a disgruntled employee who uses it as an act of revenge before leaving. More commonly, the hacker calls or emails a person who is already a user on the network and attempts to trick them into giving up their username and password.

Crikey! What Else Should I Look Out For?

Phishing attacks are very commonplace these days. These are scams whereby criminals try to convince you to give up personal information, such as your credit card number, Social Security number, passwords, and usernames. They then use this information to gain access to accounts you might have on websites like Amazon, eBay, and Apple, so they can spend all of your hard-earned money on themselves before they're spotted by your credit card company.

In the context of business, Phishing attacks might be used to gain access to a company network by pretending to be a company email requiring you to confirm your security details, or set up a new service that you need as an employee. If you work for a secure government department, or a branch of the military you may have already been briefed about this type of attack, as it's commonly used by security agencies and governments as a means of infiltration and intelligence gathering. It can also be used against research and investment firms and for industrial espionage.

Okay, Now My Head Hurts! How Do I Stay Safe?

Staying safe on your PC is actually very simple and straightforward. It just involves being vigilant about what you do on your network and online. There's so much on the Internet that's trying to take advantage of you— approaching anything that happens these days with a healthy dose of skepticism doesn't hurt either.

Keep Everything Up-to-Date

The first rule is to make sure that your PC, your antivirus software, and the apps you use are always kept up-to-date. Windows 10 takes care of itself via Windows Update, but you can manually check the status of both Windows Update, and Windows Defender on your PC by opening Settings and then clicking *Update & Security* (see Figure 9-4).

Figure 9-4. *You can check and run Windows Update manually*

If you use a third-party anti-malware package, make sure it is set to automatically update itself. Where you can check for updates in the package varies from one product to another, but it is always straightforward to find, such as with ESET Smart Security (see Figure 9-5).

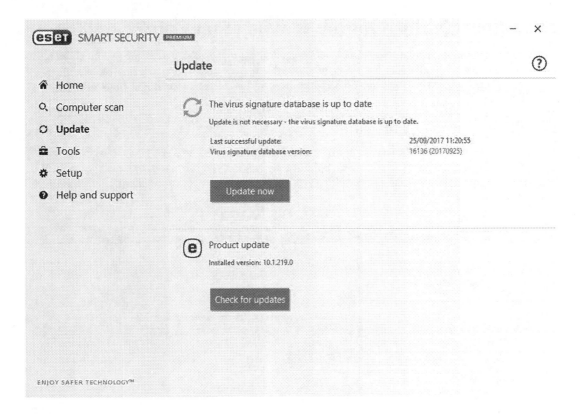

Figure 9-5. *It's always easy to update anti-malware software*

You also need to make sure that any apps and software you use on your PC is kept to up-to-date. Older and out of date apps can contain vulnerabilities that can be exploited by malware and hackers. You can update apps in one of several ways.

- Many software packages contain a button or an option that allows you to check to see if there is a newer version available (see Figure 9-6).

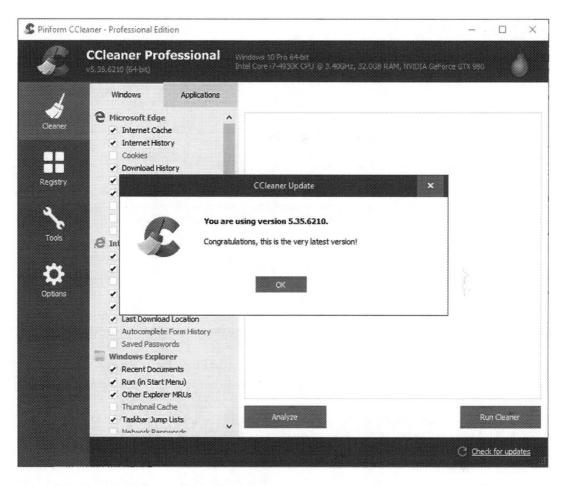

Figure 9-6. *Many apps allow you to check for updates*

- Other apps alert you when a newer version of the software is available, and then prompt you to download it.

- Some apps, such as Apple iTunes and Adobe Creative Cloud, run updater apps that sit in your system tray and update the app automatically in the background.

- Apps from the Microsoft Store are automatically updated by Windows 10 whenever a new version of an app becomes available.

- If all else fails, check the website of the company that made the software to see if updates are available. If it's discontinued software that is no longer supported, consider an alternative. A newer app will do the same thing for you.

Use Strong Passwords and Two-Factor Authentication

You should always use secure passwords on your PC, and online. I have a video online showing you how to create strong passwords, which you can find at `http://pcs.tv/2wRi3wY`, but the rules are quite simple and straightforward to follow and understand.

- **DO NOT** use dictionary words, names, or obvious passwords. Some of the most common passwords are admin, password, 12345, monkey, and password 123. All of these are easily guessable by a criminal and instantly guessable by a computer.

- **DO** use longer passwords, such as phase, line from a poem of lyric from a song. The longer the password the harder it is to guess or crack.

- **DO** mix numbers, and characters into your password. There are many good ways you can do this, such as substituting the number 5 for the letter S, using & instead of a, / instead of 7, (instead of C, () instead of o, 3 instead of E, 1 instead of i, and so on.

- **NEVER USE THE SAME PASSWORD TWICE** You should use unique passwords for each website, or web service you use. These are easily manageable because you can create a strong *core* password, and then personalize it by adding additional characters at the beginning or end of it that are unique to the website or service you're using. For example, you can use *aMa* (Amazon), *eBa* (eBay), or *sPo* (Spotify) at the end of your password where you know the added characters always form an easy to remember pattern. Or you could use a more secure format like *-AmAz()n*, which strengthens your password further by making it longer.

- **USE BIOMETRICS** if available, such as Windows Hello's facial recognition or fingerprint-reader hardware to sign in to your PC. There is a caveat with this that I will deal with shortly.

- **USE TWO-FACTOR AUTHENTICATION** if it is available, which it is on many websites and services from Microsoft to Google. This feature uses a second device, such as your smartphone to issue a single-use security code that's required when signing into the service from an unrecognized PC.

- **DO NOT** use a simple PIN to sign in to your PC. There's no point in having a super-secure password and Windows Hello to sign in to your PC if you also have an insecure four-digit PIN set up on the device. PINs can be useful in that they're never stored in the cloud, but are local to the PC, but a four-digit PIN only has 9,999 possible combinations. Windows Hello requires you set up a PIN, but Windows 10 allows you to have a PIN of any length, and one that also includes letters and other characters.

Don't Just Click Anything Online!

It's easy to be complacent when using our PCs online. It's the same feeling you can have in your car, in that you're separated from the outside world, safe and secure. The trouble is that you're really not. You're connecting to websites and servers right across the planet every time you visit a website.

Regardless of what web browser you use, Microsoft Edge, Firefox, or Google Chrome (Internet Explorer can no longer be considered safe and secure for general use) they all work in the same way to keep you safe online.

When you visit a website on which you are required to enter personal information, set up or use an account, or make a purchase, you are always shown a green padlock if the website is known to be safe and issued a security certificate. You can click this padlock icon to check that it matches the information about the site you're on (see Figure 9-7).

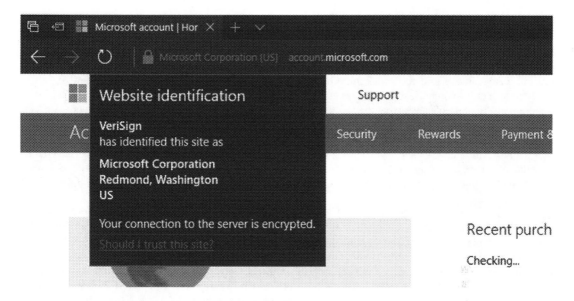

Figure 9-7. *Always look for the green padlock on websites*

If the padlock of the address bar is Red, then you are on a website that is known to be unsafe, and you should close the browser tab immediately. Additionally, if you are making a purchase online and there is no padlock icon, *stop immediately*! That website is not secure. Your information will not be encrypted when transmitted across the Internet. The purchase you are making or the account you are setting up is probably part of a scam.

Don't Click Anything in Your Email Either!

You're fully aware of the nuisance that is spam email and how it tries to sell you everything from sex aids to instant girlfriends. You wouldn't click a link in a spam email, but did you know that you should be just as wary of the emails sent by friends and colleagues?

▨ **Note** Spam email is named after a type of canned, cooked meat made from processed pork that was often eaten during and after World War II. It was widely disliked by those who had to eat it, largely because it was fatty, full of gelatin, and generally tasted disgusting. The name was later used by Monty Python in a comedy sketch in which every food available in a café had Spam in it. If you're brave enough, you can still find and buy Spam today.

Malware typically propagates itself by sending emails to everybody in any address book that it finds. These emails may contain a link that you are encouraged to click, or an attachment that you are enticed to open. If you suspect an email that you receive is fraudulent, check with the person that sent it to see if they really intended to do so.

Safety and Security Are Common Sense

Keeping your data safe is a matter of common sense. Keep Windows and your apps up-to-date, use up-to-date anti-malware software, don't disable or otherwise tamper with the security features in Windows or your anti-malware software, and don't click something just because an app, email, or website wants you to.

Part of keeping yourself safe is involves encouraging those around you to also stay safe. If you have children, you're probably aware that they look at all sorts of random rubbish online, some of which is no doubt harmful. By educating the people around you, helping and encouraging them to use best practices, you're also looking after yourself, as there will be fewer threats arriving by email and across your network.

Stopping and thinking before you click something is also essential. If you open a download or an email attachment, which then flags a UAC prompt, you could be tempted to just click OK before you stop to think about what's going on. At this point, it's already too late: if it's malware, then you've given it full administrator rights on your PC.

If you share a PC with other people, then it is very wise not to check the *Remember my username and password* option on websites, as this can additionally expose you to fraud and theft, especially if the PC is used in public places, or educational establishments such as at college.

Finally, when you connect to a Wi-Fi network and you are asked if you want other PCs on that network to be able to see your PC, only click Yes if you're on a safe home or office network. *Never* click Yes if you are in a public place, such as coffee shop or a library; doing so will mean that your PC and any files, folders, and disks on which you have sharing configured will be viewable and available to anyone in the vicinity.

Summary

It's important to remember that PC security is holistic and not confined to a specific device. A weak password on your Internet router makes your PC just as vulnerable as if it has a weak password itself. If you're tired when browsing online increase the risk that you'll click something you shouldn't, and sharing a PC with others means you don't necessarily know what they were doing on it before you were.

This isn't the end of the story, though. In the next chapter, I'll show you how to maintain a stable, reliable, and robust system on your PC that enables you to work more productively and with as little downtime as possible.

▓ ▓ ▓

CHAPTER 10

Maintaining a Stable and Reliable Working Environment

It's very difficult to get any work done or be at all productive if your PC isn't working, or isn't working reliably, or is busy installing updates. One of the issues with Windows, especially in a business environment, is the installation of Windows Updates at the most inappropriate time, which means you're sitting and twiddling your thumbs for... well, you have to guess.

There's always the lingering concern about reliability and stability with PCs. You install something—a Windows Update, a driver, a new app, or a software update. Will everything still work, and work reliably?

The good news is that Windows 10 is the most stable and reliable version of the operating system that Microsoft has ever produced. This is ironic given that it contains more support and recovery tools than any other version of Windows before it. It does mean that problems should be few and far between.

There's still things you can do to help ensure that stability and reliability, and help make sure that when Windows Updates are installed, they don't interfere with your own workflow.

If It Ain't Broke, Don't Fix It

There is a common saying: "If it ain't broke, don't fix it." It's a good methodology to follow too, although there are some notable exceptions. Generally speaking, it's a good rule to follow because if something *is* working, what's the incentive to update it and potentially cause a problem?

Where this presents a potential issue relates back to the security holes that can be present in software or hardware drivers, and how these can open your PC to malware infection or hacking.

So how do you deal with this dilemma? The easy solution is to let your software, apps and drivers update themselves. This happens through Windows Update, through the Microsoft Store app, through a standalone updater in the system tray, or through a notification when you open an app on your desktop that an update is available.

If you approach the updating of apps and drivers in this manner, then you'll know that you have a better than average chance that whatever is downloaded and installed will be stable and reliable. I'm not saying this is guaranteed as buggy software is occasionally still released, and given the almost infinite combinations of hardware and software our PCs run these days, it's a very difficult job sometimes to write code in a way you can guarantee is stable.

Taming Windows Update

Clearly one of the biggest barriers to productivity in the workplace is the message, "Windows is installing updates, don't turn off your PC." When the update installs are small and relatively minor, they won't disrupt your workflow for more than a couple of minutes.

© Mike Halsey 2017
M. Halsey, *The Windows 10 Productivity Handbook*, https://doi.org/10.1007/978-1-4842-3294-1_10

At times, however, there's a major update or a lot of smaller updates (especially if your PC was off while you were on vacation), which can prevent you from using your PC for 20 minutes or more.

There are two things that you can do to help prevent this and so that every time you return to your PC, it's updated and ready to work. You need to tame Windows Update and you need to correctly configure your power settings.

We'll deal with the former first. If you open Windows Update from the Settings app, you see the *Change active hours* link. Here you can tell Windows Update the hours that you work (see Figure 10-1), so that if an update restart is required, Windows 10 won't automatically restart ... without checking that you're using the PC.

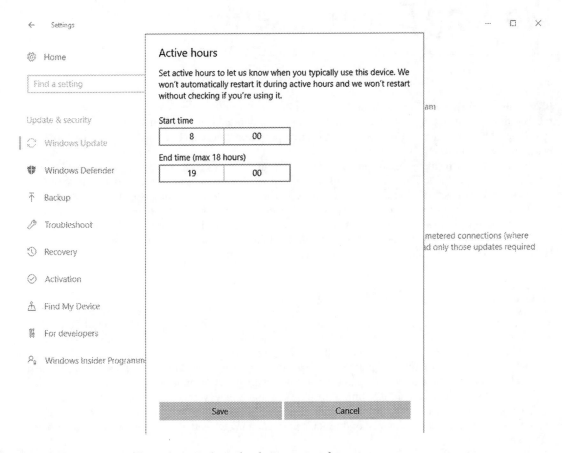

Figure 10-1. *You can tell Windows Update what hours you work*

In fairness, this is a bit of a fudge, as it doesn't in guarantee that you won't be nagged to restart the PC when you're really busy.

This is where the *Restart options* link can be useful. This allows you to configure how and when Windows 10 restarts to install an update (see Figure 10-2).

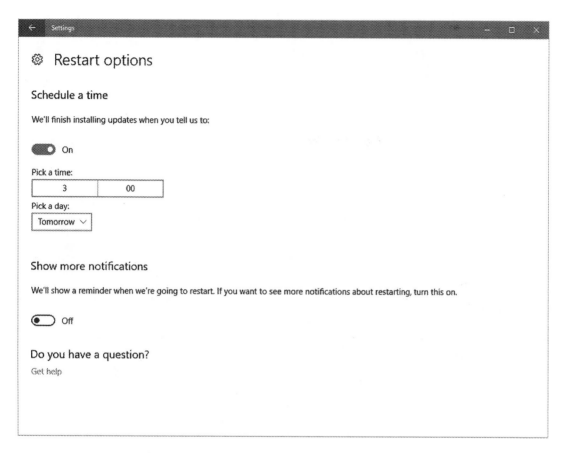

Figure 10-2. *You can configure restarts in Windows Update*

If you have a restart pending, you can use this feature to delay it until a time when you're not using the PC. You might for example set it to install automatically when you go to lunch or a meeting, or you might want to install overnight when you're guaranteed to be out of the office.

Sleeping at Work

So you want to set your PC to only install Windows Updates that require a restart overnight, when you're not at work. But whenever you leave the office, you switch off your PC because if you don't, it's using power all night.

Modern PCs are very adept at managing power effectively when you put them to sleep. This might be something you only associate with a laptop or especially a tablet, where quickly pressing the power button wakes the device up into the exact state it was when you were last using it. Desktop PCs can also take advantage of Sleep, however, which can save you valuable time when you return to work each morning.

In the Settings app, click *System* and then *Power & sleep*. Here you are presented with two single drop-down menus for when the screen turns off, and when the PC goes to sleep. On a laptop or convertible tablet, these are already configured, but on a desktop PC, you might find that the sleep option is set to Never. If you change this to, say 1 hour (see Figure 10-3), then you just leave your PC when the day ends and it automatically goes to sleep after that time, when you can wake it by hitting a key on the keyboard, tapping the screen if it's touch sensitive, or moving the mouse.

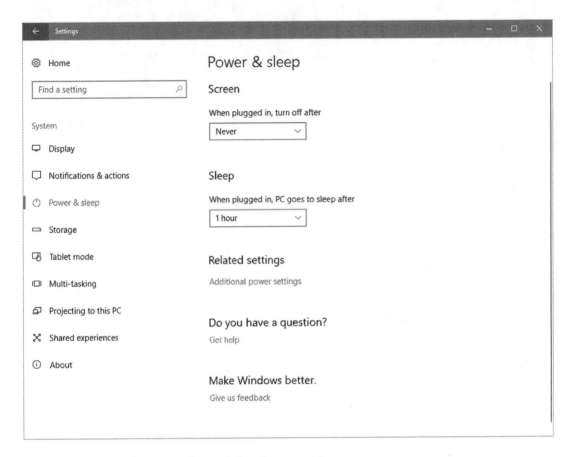

Figure 10-3. *You can set any Windows 10 PC to sleep overnight*

You don't need to worry about power consumption either as even the most powerful PC only sips small amounts of power while in Sleep. It wakes occasionally to refresh live tiles in the Start menu (if you have them) and to check for updates, and so forth; but crucially, it uses this middle-of-the-night time to install any new Windows updates, and then restarts the PC, putting it back to sleep when it's done.

▦ **Tip**   One of the advantages of putting a PC to sleep instead of switching it off at the end of the day, is that Windows Updates can be downloaded at night, when the network and your Internet bandwidth isn't used for anything else. If you have many PCs downloading updates simultaneously, this can really slow your Internet traffic and cause a chain reaction on the productivity of everybody in the workplace.

Occasionally, you'll find that a PC (often an older one) won't happily go to sleep, or won't happily wake afterward. There things you can do about this. In the *Power & sleep* settings, click the *Additional power settings* link. This opens a new window, where you see the *Choose what the power buttons do* link in its top-right corner. Click it.

The next thing to do is to click the *Change settings that are currently unavailable* link near the top center of the window. You are presented with a series of power options that you can change (see Figure 10-4).

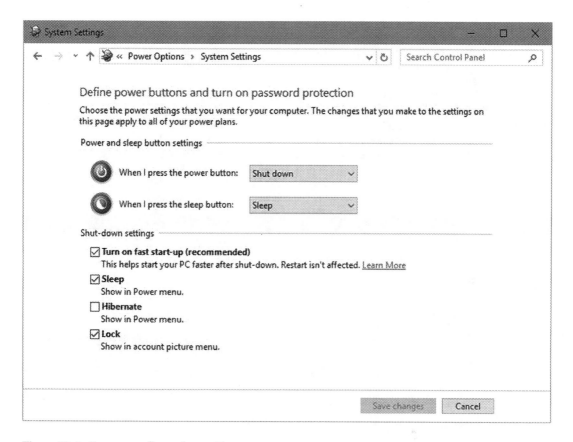

Figure 10-4. *You can configure sleep settings*

- The first two options might be worth configuring. It's not very common these days for a PC to come with a dedicated Sleep button. Only laptops tend to have them, and then only on a Fn + other key combination on the keyboard. But the Sleep feature can make your life simpler by automatically putting your PC to sleep so that you don't need to switch it off. You can still turn off your PC from the Start menu's power options when you want to, but you have a very quick-and-easy-to-use Sleep button.

- *Fast Start-up* isn't supported by all PC hardware. It is a function that saves parts of memory to the hard disk on shutdown to facilitate a slightly faster "boot from cold" speed. It is not a Sleep option, so you can safely ignore it.

- *Sleep* might be disabled on some PCs, normally older desktops. If it is disabled, there could a very good reason for it. My advice is to activate it, put the PC to sleep, and watch what happens. If it won't sleep, or won't wake when you press a key or move the mouse, then the methods I've described here won't work on that machine.

- *Hibernate* saves the contents of memory to the hard disk before shutting the PC down. It enables a faster startup, but isn't Sleep, so won't wake the PC in the night to install updates. It's been superseded by Fast start-up, and is deactivated on PCs that support that newer feature.

Pausing and Deferring Updates

Microsoft has two "channels" that allow you to defer Windows Updates. They enable system administrators to make sure that any delivered updates are stable and compatible with the software and hardware used in the workplace before installation; however, there is an added use.

Occasionally, an update from Windows Update causes a PC to become unstable, crash, or even fail to start. These instances are very rare but can occur, which is why IT administrators are always so cautious about updates. Deferring the installation of faulty updates gives Microsoft and third parties time to identify any problems, withdraw the faulty update, and issue a replacement.

If you are using Windows 10 Pro, Pro for Workstation, Enterprise, or Windows 10 S, you can choose to opt into the business channel. You do this by clicking the *Advanced options* link in the Windows Update settings (see Figure 10-5).

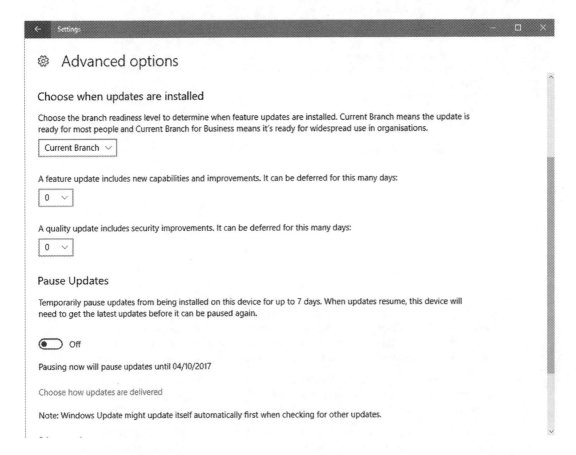

Figure 10-5. *You can defer some updates in Windows 10 Pro*

Opting into the business channel allows you to defer *some* updates for up to a year, but there are caveats, of which you need to be aware.

- Security updates can only be deferred for a maximum of 30 days, as clearly they're very important.

- New Windows 10 features and user interface enhancements can be deferred for one day to one year. Bear in mind that many new features can greatly enhance productivity, so it's often worth letting these install after 30 days.

░ **Caution**   Enterprise environments can enroll PCs on the *Long-Term Servicing Channel* (LTSC). This defers security and stability updates for up to 30 days, but can defer feature updates for up to ten years. LTSC isn't intended for standard desktop use, however. It is intended for use on mission-critical systems, such as medical scanners, automatic teller machines, and workplace machinery. As such, Microsoft Office, the Microsoft Store, and Store apps won't install or run on PCs enrolled in LTSC.

Below the option to defer updates in the Advanced Windows Update options is the *Pause Updates* button. If you're busy, working on a tight deadline (you're over yours, Ed.), or you otherwise cannot be disturbed by PC restarts and update installations, flicking this switch automatically pauses *all* new updates on the PC for a week.

Using the Automated Troubleshooters

Let's say you do encounter a problem on your PC that's making the system unstable or unreliable. There are a few things you can do that might rectify the problem. The first is to run one of the automated troubleshooters. You'll find these in the Settings app under *Update & security* ➤ *Troubleshoot* (see Figure 10-6).

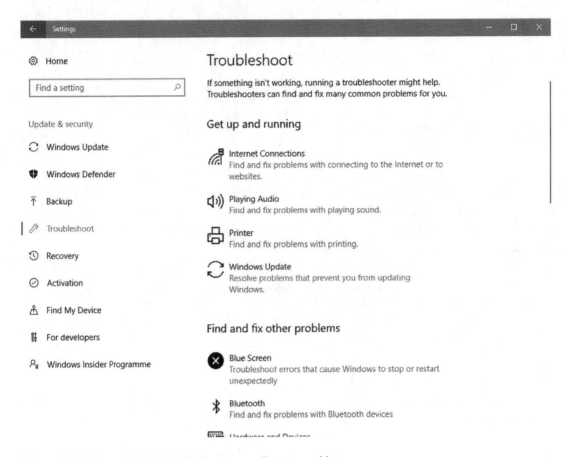

***Figure 10-6.** The automated troubleshooters can fix some problems*

The automated troubleshooters work by resetting Windows components to their standard (default) state, so they won't fix anything more complicated than a configuration snarl-up. There are quite a few of them, however, and they can prove useful.

System Restore

System Restore has been around since the days of Windows ME, when it was a favorite place for malware to hide; but in Windows 10, it's a very useful way to roll back changes that have made the PC unstable or unreliable.

If you find that a Windows update, driver, app, or other software update or configuration change is causing problems, search in the Start menu for Restore, and click the *Create a restore point* option when it appears.

This in itself is worth remembering because it's here that you can turn on/off System Restore for different hard disks on the PC. You don't need it for drives that only contain files, for example. Manually creating a restore point can be useful if you are about to make a change to the PC, but you aren't certain that doing so won't cause you any problems.

Click *Configure* to change the drives protected by *System Restore* (useful if you discover your Windows installation drive isn't protected), or click *Create* to manually create a restore point. If you want to roll back changes that have been made to Windows, your divers, updates, and apps, click the *System Restore* button (see Figure 10-7).

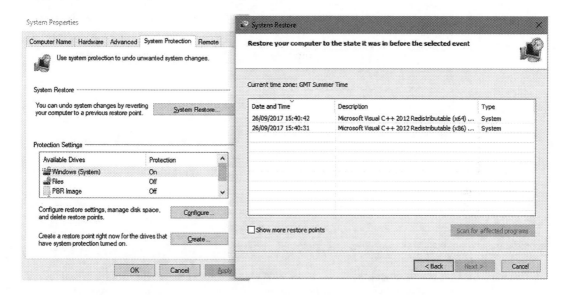

Figure 10-7. *System Restore rolls back unwanted changes*

A wizard opens to show you a list of available and recently created restore points. Each one has the date, time, and a brief description of what triggered the automatic (or manual) creation.

Windows 10 shows you the most recent available restore points, but there may be more from which you can choose. For example, if you have experienced trouble since an update was installed a week ago, you can select the *Show more restore points* check box to see if any others are available.

Once you have chosen a restore point, you can click the *Scan for affected programs* button, which displays a list all programs and drivers that will be rolled back to a previous version, or perhaps even deleted when you start the Restore. You might find that choosing a particular restore point has an undesirable effect. You may want to see if a more appropriate restore point is available instead.

Creating a Windows 10 Recovery Drive

Sometimes you might find that something goes so wrong with the PC that it won't start, or is regularly suffering from a Blue Screen of Death. If you need to run System Restore but can't reliably get access to the Windows desktop, you can instead do this from a USB *recovery drive*. To create one, you need a spare USB flash drive that you're not using for anything else of at least 4GB in size. In the Start menu, search for **recovery** and open the *Recovery (Control Panel)* option when you see it.

A window will appear, in which the first option is to *Create a recovery drive*. Click this and a wizard will appear on the screen (see Figure 10-8).

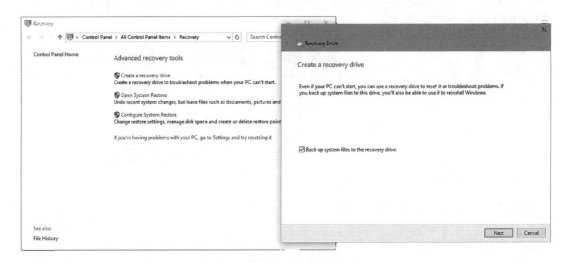

Figure 10-8. *You can create a USB recovery drive*

This wizard guides you through the process of creating a USB recovery drive. That drive can then be used to start the PC into the Windows Recovery Environment if it won't start, or won't start reliably. Note that you need to have your PC set to allow "booting from USB" and you should check the manual that came with the PC for how to do this.

There is an additional option that may or may not be available on your PC. This is the *Back up system files to the recovery drive* check box. If you check this option, it copies a full backup image of your Windows installation so that if something goes horribly wrong, you can still restore your copy of Windows. Note that this Reset option, which is also available in the *Update & security* ➤ *Recovery* section of the Settings app, requires you to reinstall all of your software and apps.

To use this option, you need a much larger USB flash drive—at least 8GB (possibly up to 32GB)—to accommodate the space required for the backup copy of Windows 10.

Either way, a recovery drive is an incredibly useful thing to have, and I always recommend that one be created for each PC. The reason to have one for each machine is because not all recovery drives can be used to rescue all versions of Windows, as Windows editions tend to vary, and require different things from a recovery drive. Also, because of hardware driver support, a reset image from one PC cannot be used to rescue Windows 10 on another PC.

░ **Tip**   The Reset option in Windows 10 reinstalls the operating system without affecting your files, accounts, or settings, although you have to reinstall all your software and apps. However, it also comes with an option to wipe the PC completely. This is not a secure wipe, so an experienced IT engineer could still recover files and data, but it's a useful tool if you're passing a PC on to another person such as a family member.

Summary

There's no point in making yourself as productive as you can be if your PC is unreliable and unresponsive. This chapter has guided through the tools it's easiest for you to use yourself, but others are also available. If you feel a bit more ambitious and technically minded, you can find all the information you need to diagnose, troubleshoot, and repair problems in Windows 10 in my book *Windows 10 Troubleshooting* (Apress, 2016), which you can find online at `http://pcs.tv/2wWbdWP` and at good booksellers.

Armed with the information in this book, you can be more productive, happier, and most importantly, more confident that you can do all the great things that you've seen friends and colleagues do—and a lot more besides. I encourage you to keep learning and perhaps to also read my *Office 365 Productivity Handbook* (Apress, 2018) next!

APPENDIX A

Windows 10 Shortcut Keys

Table A-1. *Keys with No Modifier*

Key	Function
Space	Selects or clears the active check box
Tab	Moves forward through the options
Esc	Cancel
NumLock	Holds for 5 seconds: ToggleKeys
Del	Deletes the file (File Explorer)
Left arrow	Opens the previous menu or close submenu
Right arrow	Opens the next menu of the open submenu
F1	Displays help (if available)
F2	Renames the item
F3	Searches for the next instance in a search
F4	Displays the items in active list
F5	Refresh

Table A-2. *Windows Logo Key Combinations*

Windows Logo Key+	Function
No other key	Toggles the Start menu
PrtScr	Capture screenshot (saved in Pictures as screenshot.png, screenshot(1).png, screenshot(2).png, etc.)
A	Opens the Action Center
C	Opens Cortana Voice Input
D	Adds a virtual desktop
E	Opens File Explorer
H	Opens Share flyout
I	Opens the Settings app
J	Switches the focus between snapped and larger apps
K	Opens the Connect to Devices flyout

(continued)

© Mike Halsey 2017

M. Halsey, *The Windows 10 Productivity Handbook*, https://doi.org/10.1007/978-1-4842-3294-1

Table A-2. (*continued*)

Windows Logo Key+	Function
L	Switches users (lock computer if on a domain)
M	Minimizes all windows (desktop)
O	Changes the lock-screen orientation
P	Opens the second screen and projection options
Q	Opens the Full Cortana dialog
R	Opens the Run dialog box
T	Sets focus on the taskbar and cycle through running desktop programs
U	Opens the Ease of Access Center
V	Cycles through notifications (+Shift to go backward)
X	Opens the Administration Commands menu
1-9	Goes to the app at the position on the taskbar
+	Zooms in (Magnifier)
-	Zooms out (Magnifier)
, (comma)	Peeks at the desktop
Enter	Narrator (+Alt to open the Windows Media Center, if installed)
Spacebar	Switches input language and keyboard layout
Tab	Opens Task View
Esc	Exits the Magnifier
Home	Minimizes nonactive desktop windows
Left arrow	Snaps the window to the left (+Shift to move to the left monitor)
Left arrow, plus hold Win + Up Arrow	Snaps the window to the top-left corner or screen
Left arrow, plus hold Win + Down Arrow	Snaps the window to bottom-left corner of the screen
Right arrow	Snaps the windows to the right (+Shift to move to the right monitor)
Right arrow, plus hold Win + Up arrow	Snaps the window to top-right corner of the screen
Right arrow, plus hold Win + Down arrow	Snaps the window to the bottom-right corner of the screen
Shift + Left	Moves an app to the monitor on the left
Shift + Right	Moves an app to the monitor on the right
Ctrl + Left	Switches to the virtual desktop on the left
Ctrl + Right	Switches to the virtual desktop on the right
Ctrl + F4	Closes the current virtual desktop
Up arrow	Maximizes the desktop window (+Shift to keep width)
Down arrow	Restores/Minimizes the desktop window (+Shift to keep width)
F1	Opens Windows Help and Support in a browser

Table A-3. *Ctrl Key Combinations*

Ctrl+	Function
Mouse wheel	Desktop: Change icon size, Start screen: Zoom in/out
A	Select All
C	Copy
E	Select search box (Explorer)
N	New window (Explorer)
R	Refresh
V	Paste
W	Close current window (Explorer)
X	Cut
Y	Redo
Z	Undo
Esc	Start screen
NumLock	Copy
Left arrow	Previous word
Right arrow	Next word
Up arrow	Previous paragraph
Down arrow	Next paragraph
F4	Close active document

Table A-4. *Alt Key Combinations*

Alt+	Function
D	Selects the address bar (Explorer)
Enter	Opens the Properties dialog box
Spacebar	Opens Shortcut menu
Tab	Switches between apps
Left arrow	Moves to previous folder (Explorer)
Up arrow	Goes up one level (Explorer)
F4	Closes the active item or app

Table A-5. *Shift Key Combinations*

Shift+	Function
No other key	Five times: Sticky keys
Tab	Move backward through options
Esc	Open the Task Manager
NumLock	Paste
Left arrow	Selects a block of text
Right arrow	Selects a block of text
Up arrow	Selects a block of text
Down arrow	Selects a block of text

Table A-6. *Ctrl + Alt Key Combinations*

Ctrl + Alt+	Function
D	Toggle Docked mode (Magnifier)
I	Invert colors (Magnifier)
L	Toggle Lens mode (Magnifier)
Tab	Switch between apps using arrow keys

Table A-7. *Alt + Shift Key Combinations*

Alt + Shift+	Function
PrtScr	Left Alt + Left Shift + PrtScr: High contrast
NumLock	Left Alt + Left Shift + NumLock: Mouse keys

APPENDIX B

■ ■ ■

Windows 10 Touch and Trackpad Gestures

For many people, touch will be new to their Windows experience. In many ways, such as with tapping and double-tapping, touch operates in the same way that you expect a mouse-click to work. Table B-1 is a complete list of the touch gestures that you can use with Windows 10. Those who already use touch will be pleased to hear that the gestures haven't changed.

Table B-1. *Windows 10 Touch Gestures*

Touch Gesture	Command	Action
Tap	Click	Tap the screen with your finger.
Double tap	Double-click	Tap the screen twice in the same place with your finger.
Drag vertically	Scroll	Touch the screen and vertically drag your finger upward or downward.
Drag horizontally	Drag selection	Touch the screen and horizontally drag your finger left or right.
Press and hold	Right-click	Touch and hold the screen with one finger while tapping it briefly with another finger.
Zoom	Zoom	Move two fingers apart (zoom in) or toward each other (zoom out).
Rotate	Rotate	Move two fingers in a circular motion.
Two-finger tap	Programmable in some apps	Tap the screen with two fingers.
Flick	Pan up, down, back, forward	Flick your finger up, down, left, or right on the screen.
Swipe from left of screen	Open Task View	Swipe inward from the left bezel of your screen.
Swipe from right of screen	Open Action Center	Swipe inward from the right bezel of your screen.

© Mike Halsey 2017

M. Halsey, *The Windows 10 Productivity Handbook*, https://doi.org/10.1007/978-1-4842-3294-1

Narrator Touch Gestures

The Accessibility features in Windows have long been a strength of the operating system, but in Windows 10, they have been extended to add support for touch gestures that work with the Narrator. In Table B-2, the touch gesture listed in the left column executes the corresponding command in the right column.

Table B-2. *Narrator Touch Gestures*

Touch Gesture	Command
Tap or drag	Read aloud the item under your finger.
Double tap or Hold with one finger and tap with a second finger	Activate an item (equivalent to a single mouse-click).
Triple tap or Hold with one finger and double-tap with a second finger	Select an item.
Flick left or right	Move to the next or previous item.
Hold with one finger and two-finger-tap with additional fingers	Drag an item.
Two-finger tap	Stop the Narrator.
Two-finger swipe	Scroll.
Three-finger tap	Show or hide the Narrator settings window.
Three-finger swipe up	Read the current window.
Three-finger swipe down	Read from the current text location.
Three-finger swipe left or right	Tab forward and backward.
Four-finger tap	Show all commands for the current item.
Four-finger triple tap	Show the Narrator commands list.
Four-finger swipe up or down	Enable/disable semantic zoom (semantic zoom provides a view of large blocks of content; on a web site, for example).

Trackpad Gestures

Windows 10 includes gestures that can be used on a laptop's or an Ultrabook's trackpad (see Table B-3). These are performed by simultaneously using multiple fingers on the trackpad.

Table B-3. *Windows 10 Trackpad Gestures*

Touch Gesture	Command
Swipe downward with three fingers	Show desktop
Swipe upward with three fingers	Undo Show Desktop
Swipe upward with three fingers	Open Task View
Swipe three fingers left or right	Switch between open apps

APPENDIX C

■ ■ ■

Advanced Query Syntax for Search

In addition to the search methods that I detailed in Chapter 5, there is a large volume of Advanced Query Syntax options that you can use when searching (especially for files) in Windows 10. These options are available both at the Start screen and in File Explorer, see Tables C-1 to C-16.

Data Store Location

Table C-1. *Data Store Location*

Restrict Search by Data Store	Use	Example
Desktop	desktop	Gilbert store:desktop
Files	files	Mike store:files
Outlook	outlook	Jed store:outlook
A specific folder	foldername or in	foldername:MyDocuments or in:MyVideos

© Mike Halsey 2017
M. Halsey, *The Windows 10 Productivity Handbook*, https://doi.org/10.1007/978-1-4842-3294-1

Common File Types

Table C-2. Common File Types

Restrict Search by File Type	Use	Example
Calendar	calendar	kind:=calendar
Communication	communication	kind:=communication
Contact	contact	kind:=contact
Document	document	kind:=document
Email	email	kind:=email
RSS Feed	feed	kind:=feed
Folder	folder	kind:=folder
Game	game	kind:=game
Instant Messenger conversations	instant message	kind:=instant message
Journal	journal	kind:=journal
Link	link	kind:=link
Movie	movie	kind:=movie
Music	music	kind:=music
Notes	note	kind:=note
Picture	picture	kind:=picture
Playlist	playlist	kind:=playlist
Program	program	kind:=program
Recorded TV	tv	kind:=tv
Saved search	saved search	kind:=saved search
Task	task	kind:=task
Video	video	kind:=video
Web history	web history	kind:=web history

Properties by File Type

Table C-3. *Properties by File Type*

Property	Use	Example
Title	title, subject or about	title:"Windows 10"
Status	status	status:pending
Date	date	date:last week
Date modified	datemodified or modified	modified:last week
Importance	importance or priority	importance:high
Deleted	deleted or isdeleted	isdeleted:yes (no)
Is attachment	isattachment	isattachment:yes (no)
To	to or toname	to:mike
Cc	cc or ccname	cc:chris
Company	company	company:Microsoft
Location	location	location:"office"
Category	category	category:pilot
Keywords	keywords	keywords:"pending"
Album	album	album:"equinoxe"
File name	filename or file	filename:Report
Genre	genre	genre:metal
Author	author or by	author:"Mike Halsey"
People	people or with	with:(jed or gilbert)
Folder	folder, under or path	folder:downloads
File extension	ext or fileext	ext:.txt

Filter by Size

Table C-4. *Filter by Size (Note that the NOT and OR operators must be in uppercase.)*

Size	Use	Example
0KB	empty	size:empty
0 > 10KB	tiny	size:tiny
10KB > 100KB	small	size:small
100KB > 1MB	medium	size:medium
1MB > 16MB	large	size:large
16MB > 128MB	huge	size:huge
> 128MB	gigantic	size:gigantic

Boolean Operators

Table C-5. *Boolean Operators (Note that the NOT and OR operators here must be in uppercase.)*

Keyword/Symbol	Use	Function
NOT	draft NOT edition	Finds items that contain *draft*, but not *edition*.
–	draft –edition	Finds items that contain *draft*, but not *edition*.
OR	draft OR edition	Finds items that contain *draft* or *edition*.
Quotation marks	"draft edition"	Finds items that contain the exact phrase *draft edition*.
Parentheses	(draft edition)	Finds items that contain *draft* and *edition* in any order.
>	date:>10/23/12	Finds items with a date after October 23, 2015.
	size:>500	Finds items with a size greater than 500 bytes.
<	date:<10/23/12	Finds items with a date before October 23, 2015.
	size:<500	Finds items with a size less than 500 bytes.
..	date:10/23/12..10/11/12	Finds items with a date beginning on 10/23/12 and ending on 10/11/12.

Boolean Properties

Table C-6. *Boolean Properties*

Property	Use	Function
is:attachment	draft is:attachment	Finds items that have attachments that contain *draft*. Same as isattachment:no (yes).
isonline:	draft isonline:yes (no)	Finds items that are online and that contain *draft*.
isrecurring:	draft isrecurring:yes (no)	Finds items that are recurring and that contain *draft*.
isflagged:	draft isflagged:yes (no)	Finds items that are flagged (Review or Follow up, for example) and that contain *draft*.
isdeleted:	draft isdeleted:yes (no)	Finds items that are flagged as deleted (Recycle Bin or Deleted Items, for example) and that contain *draft*.
iscompleted:	draft iscompleted:yes (no)	Finds items that are not flagged as complete and that contain *draft*.
hasattachment:	draft hasattachment:yes (no)	Finds items containing *draft* and having attachments.
hasflag:	draft hasflag:yes (no)	Finds items containing *draft* and having flags.

Dates

Table C-7. *Dates*

Relative to	Use	Function
Day	date:today	Finds items with today's date
	date:tomorrow	Finds items with tomorrow's date
	date:yesterday	Finds items with yesterday's date
Week/Month/Year	date:this week	Finds items with a date falling within the current week
	date:last week	Finds items with a date falling within the previous week
	date:next month	Finds items with a date falling within the upcoming week
	date:last month	Finds items with a date falling within the previous month
	date:this year	Finds items with a date falling within the current year
	date:last year	Finds items with a date falling within the next year

Attachments

Table C-8. *Attachments*

Property	Use	Example
People	people	people:gilbert

Contacts

Table C-9. *Contacts*

Property	Use	Example
Job title	jobtitle	jobtitle:author
Instant messaging address	imaddress	imaddress:mike@MVPs.org
Assistant's phone	assistantsphone	assistantsphone:555-1234
Assistant's name	assistantname	assistantname:Darren
Profession	profession	profession:designer
Nickname	nickname	nickname:Gilby
Spouse	spouse	spouse:Victoria
Business city	businesscity	businesscity:Seattle
Business postal code	businesspostalcode	businesspostalcode:96487
Business home page	businesshomepage	businesshomepage: www.thelongclimb.com
Callback phone number	callbackphonenumber	callbackphonenumber:555-555-2345
Mobile phone	mobilephone	mobilephone:555-555-2345
Children	children	children:Gilbert
First name	firstname	firstname:Jed
Last name	lastname	lastname:Halsey
Home fax	homefax	homefax:555-555-1234
Manager's name	managersname	managersname:Tom
Business phone	businessphone	businessphone:555-555-1234
Home phone	homephone	homephone:555-555-1234
Mobile phone	mobilephone	mobilephone:555-555-1234
Office	office	office:sample
Anniversary	anniversary	anniversary:1/8/94
Birthday	birthday	birthday:1/8/81
Web page	webpage	webpage: www.thelongclimb.com

Communications

Table C-10. *Communications*

Property	Use	Example
From	from or organizer	from:Jed
Received	received or sent	sent:yesterday
Subject	subject or title	subject:"Editing Report"
Has attachment	hasattachments, hasattachment	hasattachment:true
Attachments	attachments or attachment	attachment:presentation.ppt
Bcc	bcc, bccname or bccaddress	bcc:Gilbert
Cc address	ccaddress or cc	ccaddress:mike@MVPs.org
Follow-up flag	followupflag	followupflag:2
Due date	duedate or due	due:last week
Read	read or isread	is:read
Is completed	iscompleted	is:completed
Incomplete	incomplete or isincomplete	is:incomplete
Has flag	hasflag or isflagged	has:flag
Duration	duration	duration:> 50

Calendar

Table C-11. *Calendar*

Property	Use	Example
Recurring	recurring	recurring:yes (no)
Organizer	organizer, by or from	organizer:Rory

Documents

Table C-12. *Documents*

Property	Use	Example
Comments	comments	comments:"needs final review"
Last saved by	lastsavedby	lastsavedby:mike
Document manager	documentmanager	documentmanager:mike
Revision number	revisionnumber	revisionnumber:1.0.3
Document format	documentformat	documentformat:MIMETYPE
Date last printed	datelastprinted	datelastprinted:last week

Presentations

Table C-13. *Presentations*

Property	Use	Example
Slide count	slidecount	slidecount:>20

Music

Table C-14. *Music*

Property	Use	Example
Bit rate	bitrate , rate	bitrate:192
Artist	artist, by or from	artist:Lacuna Coil
Duration	duration	duration:3
Album	album	album:"shallow life"
Genre	genre	genre:metal
Track	track	track:12
Year	year	year:> 2006 < 2016

Pictures

Table C-15. *Pictures*

Property	Use	Example
Camera make	cameramake	cameramake:sample
Camera model	cameramodel	cameramodel:sample
Dimensions	dimensions	dimensions:8×10
Orientation	orientation	orientation:landscape
Date taken	datetaken	datetaken:yesterday
Width	width	width:1600
Height	height	height:1200

Video

Table C-16. *Video*

Property	Use	Example
Name	name, subject	name:"Family holiday in Germany"
Ext	ext, fileext	ext:.avi

Index

A

Accounts panel, 87
Action Center, 39
Advanced Query Syntax (AQS) search
    attachments, 123
    Boolean operator and properties, 122
    calendar, 125
    communications, 125
    configuration, 56–57
    contacts, 124
    data store location, 119
    dates, 123
    documents, 125
    File Explorer, 55–56
    file types
        commom types, 120
        properties, 121
    filter by size, 121
    libraries
        arrange by options, 59–60
        Details pane button, 61
        documents by tags, 60
        Navigation pane button, 58
        View tab, 58
    music, 126
    pictures, 126
    presentations, 126
    Quick access view, 63–65
    saved searches, 56
    sharing files and documents, 62–63
    video, 126
Automated troubleshooters, 105–106

B

Battery saver mode, 72
Boolean operators, 122
Brute-force attack, 92

C

Computer security
    administrator rights, 98
    antivirus installation
        credit card company, 92
        hacking, 92
        Malware infections, 90–92
    fraud and theft, 98
    PCs online, 96–97
    spam email, 97
    strong passwords, 96
    two-factor authentication, 96
    update & security, 93–95
Cortana
    Connected Accounts settings, 25
    films, 23
    home and work locations, 24
    intelligent reminders, 24–25
    IoT devices, 25
    OneDrive, 34
    printers, 33
    restaurants, 25
    snap, 29
    stock price value, 23
    timeline, 32
    virtual desktops, 31
    Windows Ink Workspace, 27

D, E, F, G

Devices, 9
Disk encryption technologies, 75

H

Hardware devices
    default printers, 80
    USB device, 82

■ I, J, K, L, M

Internet of Things (IoT) devices, 25
Internet Service Provider (ISP), 83

■ N, O

Narrator touch gestures, 116
Natural language search, 9
Network and Internet, 9
    Data usage option, 84
    Flight mode, 84
    mobile hotspot, 84
    VPNs, 83
    Wi-Fi settings, 83
Night light, 7, 69

■ P

Personalization
    accessibility features, 17
    background wallpaper, 14
    changing colors, 15–16
    date and time settings, 21
    desktop and window animations, 19
    keyboard options, 18
    light and dark windows themes, 20
    lock screen, 13–14
    Night light, 19
    syncing, 22
    text scaling option, 17
Productivity
    Additional power settings, 45
    app/task, 37
    display alerts and pop-up menus, 38
    Mobility Center, 46
    smart search, 45
    thumbnail image, 37–38

■ Q

Quiet hours, 39

■ R

Reliability and stability
    automated troubleshooters, 105–106
    Microsoft Store app, 99
    potential issue, 99
    recovery drive, 107–108
    System Restore, 106–107
    Windows Updates
        change active hours link, 100
        pausing and deferring, 105

    Restart options, 100–101
    sleeping at work, 101–103

■ S

Security, 85
Snap, 76–77
Solid state disk (SSD), 33
System Restore, 106–107
System settings
    multiple display settings, 70
    notifications, 71
    power and sleep settings, 75

■ T

Tablets, 76
Touch gestures, 115
Trackpad gestures, 117

■ U

User Account Control (UAC), 90

■ V

Virtual desktops, 29, 76–77
Virtual private networks (VPNs), 83

■ W, X, Y, Z

Windows 10
    Advanced Query Syntax options (*see* Advanced
        Query Syntax options)
    Alt Key, 113
    Alt + Shift Key, 114
    Control Panel, 69
    Cortana. Cortana
    Ctrl + Alt Key, 114
    Ctrl Key, 113
    default applications, 86–87
    desktop, 2–4
    Jump List features, 53
    keys with no modifier, 111
    live tiles, 4
    lock screen, 2, 49
    Logo Key, 111–112
    Narrator, 116
    Netflix episode, 7
    Personalization options (*see* Personalization)
    power savings, 7
    productivity boost (*see* Productivity)
    reliability and stability (*see* Reliability and
        stability)

security (*see* Computer security)
Settings app, 10
Shift Key, 114
sign-in methods, 2
Start menu, 4–5
taskbar, 7
touch gestures, 115
trackpad gestures, 117

traditional application, 7
virtual desktops
    Groove Music app, 50
    management, 50–51
    Outlook, 50
    web browser, 50
    word document, 50
workspace, 49

Get the eBook for only $5!

Why limit yourself?

With most of our titles available in both PDF and ePUB format, you can access your content wherever and however you wish—on your PC, phone, tablet, or reader.

Since you've purchased this print book, we are happy to offer you the eBook for just $5.

To learn more, go to http://www.apress.com/companion or contact support@apress.com.

Apress®

Printed in the United States
By Bookmasters